IN CONVERSATION WITH THE STARS

IN CONVERSATION WITH THE STARS

ANUPAMA CHOPRA

RUPA

Published by
Rupa Publications India Pvt. Ltd 2019
7/16, Ansari Road, Daryaganj
New Delhi 110002

Sales Centres:
Allahabad Bengaluru Chennai
Hyderabad Jaipur Kathmandu
Kolkata Mumbai

Copyright © Anupama Chopra 2019

Photo courtesy: *Film Companion*

The views and opinions expressed in this book are the author's own and the facts are as reported by her which have been verified to the extent possible, and the publishers are not in any way liable for the same.

All rights reserved.

No part of this publication may be reproduced, transmitted, or stored in a retrieval system, in any form or by any means, electronic, mechanical, photocopying, recording or otherwise, without the prior permission of the publisher.

ISBN: 978-93-5333-518-2

First impression 2019

10 9 8 7 6 5 4 3 2 1

The moral right of the author has been asserted.

Printed at Parksons Graphics Pvt. Ltd, Mumbai

This book is sold subject to the condition that it shall not, by way of trade or otherwise, be lent, resold, hired out, or otherwise circulated, without the publisher's prior consent, in any form of binding or cover other than that in which it is published.

Contents

Introduction   *vii*

On Combustive Performance   1
   Ranveer Singh

The Pursuit of Beauty   15
   Sanjay Leela Bhansali

Fearless Women   43
   Anushka Sharma

The Radical Royal   62
   Saif Ali Khan

Beneath the Surface   81
   Shah Rukh Khan

On Dominating the World   107
   Priyanka Chopra

Undiluted and Unstoppable   117
   Kangana Ranaut

On Bold and Unusual Choices 133
    Varun Dhawan, Anushka Sharma,
    Sriram Raghavan and Navdeep Singh

The Prince of Bollywood 150
    Ranbir Kapoor

Unfinished 166
    Hrithik Roshan

Unleashing the Hurricane 189
    Abhishek Bachchan

Introduction

What makes a great conversation? I believe it is curiosity, generosity and authenticity. The interviewer must bring a genuine passion and insight to the questions, which then enables the interviewee to reply without discomfort, hesitation or even boredom. I've been interviewing artists for over twenty-five years, and one of my favourite stories is from a chat I had with Mr Amitabh Bachchan. It was for a print publication. By this time, Mr Bachchan had already been fielding media questions for more than four decades. He was detailing for me his day, which began at 5 or 6 a.m. at the gym and ended around midnight, after he finished his daily blog. I asked in astonishment, 'When do you sleep?' He replied with a straight face, 'During interviews.' Since then, my first task during an interview has been to make sure that my subject isn't falling asleep!

The interviews you are going to read were done for *Film Companion*. This year, the platform (www.filmcompanion.in) celebrates its fifth anniversary. The name *Film Companion* was inspired by American philosopher Stanley Cavell, who said, 'The writing about film that has meant most to me has the power of a missing companion. Our aim is to be the missing companion for smart people who like good content. The platform was launched on 28 July 2014 with a video essay, titled, 'Can Salman Khan Act? Maybe. Does he need to? No'.

Since then, the attempt has been to ask provocative questions and unearth insightful, engaging answers, to be informative and entertaining—not just in interviews but also in reviews, features and analysis. We are now about so much more than film—over the years, we started to cover short films, shows on streaming platforms, cinema books, comedy, music. We added regional languages—in March 2017, and launched *Film Companion South*, led by the National Award-winning critic Baradwaj Rangan. Baradwaj and his team tackle Tamil, Telugu, Malayalam and Kannada cinema. In 2018, we started reviewing Bengali cinema. In the same year, we kicked off *Film Companion Hindi* on YouTube. Our journalistic beats, audience and ambitions kept growing.

Despite the acceleration on all fronts, our core remains the same—we are driven by a passion for cinema and storytelling. We have an insatiable curiosity about the creative process. We want to dive deeper into the instincts and methods of artists. In this book, you will get a glimpse into the minds of actors and directors—from Sanjay Leela Bhansali to Shah Rukh Khan—they are all here. The hope is to capture a time and a place so that you get an insight not just into a singular sensibility but also into an ethos.

Cinema permeates and punctuates every facet of our life—from our innermost fantasies to the way we dress, and the songs we listen to. For me, films, and especially Hindi films, have never been just entertainment. They are a way of life. I hope this book enriches your experience of cinema. Eventually, we are all film lovers. And may our tribe increase.

Anupama Chopra

On Combustive Performance

Ranveer Singh

We met Ranveer Singh a day after the release of *Padmaavat*, which at the time was his biggest box office opening yet. Ranveer's portrayal of the ruthless Alauddin Khilji made the film come alive. Many would agree that he was the heartbeat of the film. He is an entertainer—even if there is an audience of one—which is why it's such fun to listen to him.

In our conversation, he talks about *Padmaavat*, how he got into the headspace of Khilji, and how playing a villainous character was like 'Diwali cleaning of the aura'.

AC: I was just told that *Padmaavat* is your biggest opening yet.
RS: Apparently so.

AC: And honestly, Ranveer, for me, and I think for a lot of people, you are really the heartbeat of the film. You really made it come alive.
RS: Thank you.

AC: So I'll start with something that Javier Bardem had once said. He had played a terrifying villain in films such as *No Country for Old Men* and, of course, *Skyfall*. I did an interview with him where I asked him...
RS: What? You met him?

AC: Yes.
RS: You got a picture?

AC: No, we are not allowed to...
RS: He is so sexy.

AC: He really is. I agree.
RS: What about the wine he sips in Vicky Cristina Barcelona? Goals!

AC: Yes. And I asked him, do you have to like the characters you play, and he said to me, 'I don't have to like them, but I've to be able to defend them like a lawyer defends a client.' Is that true? And can you defend Alauddin Khilji?
RS: I kind of disagree. When I am playing Alauddin Khilji, what I am doing is the right thing from my perspective and point of view as Khilji. I can judge him as Ranveer and say that's wrong or that's not nice, or that's not cool. But when I am playing Alauddin, I am convinced of my purpose and my reality. I am convinced that I am the second Alexander and that I am meant to rule the world and that everything that the Almighty has created belongs to me. I have to be convinced of that. Only then can I play it convincingly on screen.

AC: What I would like to know is, how does an artist get into the headspace of this completely unhinged character, who is a stalker and a murderer? What did you read? What did you watch? How did you get there?
RS: I am not sure how much of my process I am comfortable revealing. Let's put it this way, I take some time to prepare. It

becomes very difficult to carve out time to prep in the midst of our hectic schedules. My business managers most certainly don't get it. They have to be explained that I need this time to hone my craft.

AC: Normally, how long do you take?
RS: A minimum of two weeks for me. If I get four, nothing like it. This time I got three weeks. I was in my workshop, which is in a far-off suburb, away from friends and family.

AC: Completely alone?
RS: Yes, completely alone. I isolate myself for those three weeks and I dwell in that character, sort of marinade in that headspace. And some things suddenly come to me. It's a fascinating process that doesn't have any rules; it doesn't have any set pattern. Prepping for every character is different for me. The time that I spend with myself is...it could be bizarre, if you view it from an outsider's point of view. My process is all about spending time with myself and finding that something inside me that I will need to tap into to play that character. It's a very fulfilling process.

AC: Really?
RS: Yes. And I love it. It's like you are groping in the dark. You are grabbing, you are trying to find, explore and then you arrive at some sort of base that you can take with you to the set. It's different with every director. Some like to be very hands-on and be a part of the process, so they know you are on the right track.

AC: What was it like for this film?
RS: Mr Bhansali was never involved during my prep. In fact, he had packed me off to Gujarat during *Goliyon Ki Rasleela: Ram-Leela* for my prep. I did the same thing, immersing in myself at a suburban hotel for weeks on end for *Bajirao Mastani*, and this time in my workshop. So he is very hands-off in his approach.

AC: So you enter the space, you isolate yourself from the world and when you come out, you become that character?

RS: Yeah, I find something to work with. I find a starting point, like a foundation. It was different in *Bajirao Mastani*. For Bajirao, I built the base and I was operating out of what I discovered in that base that I had created even on set. But this time, I built the base but took it to the set and let Mr Bhansali's creative genius play with it. He wanted to do so many things, and he was just brilliant. His ideas, the nuances that he added…they really enriched the depth of my character. It was very different. All three films with Mr Bhansali have been different.

AC: But Ranveer, tell me this, how much of this man was in the script and how much of it was you turning into Khilji? For instance, I love the scene where you say to Ratan Singh, 'Aap kitne acche hain (You are so nice),' and you are mocking him! You really voiced all our feelings as viewers.

RS: That was an improvisation!

AC: Yeah, exactly. So something like that can spring out of the moment instead of being a part of the script?

RS: I think, at some point, after two weeks, three weeks or sometimes even less, you find the character and then you can flow freely and then you can improvise. It happened a lot with Jim Sarbh who was playing Malik Kafur. He and I improvised a lot. But that one moment that you speak of was an improvisation because we were rehearsing the scene and Shahid (Kapoor) was saying his dialogues and I felt that sentiment and I voiced it. And Mr Bhansali was like, 'Say it! Say it in so many words.'

AC: Yeah, because at that point that man is self-righteous to the point of being destructive.

RS: To a fault.

AC: Yes, to a fault. Tell me about the scenes with Jim, because they are funny. I had problems with the whole track because I

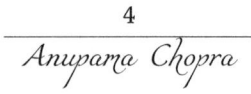

thought the very fact that you are commenting on his bisexuality is also a value judgement. You are showing it as one more sign that he is a bad guy. However, there were moments of tenderness as well. There was this lovely scene where you touch his cheek. How did you and Jim mutually agree on what you can or cannot do, since these are very sensitive things?
RS: Well, Jim is full of ideas and full of beans and actually wanted to do a lot more. Mr Bhansali had to control him and curb his enthusiasm. I have to say, it has been one of the most fulfilling co-actor experiences of my life. Jim is an absolute delight! In fact, he and I both wanted to do a lot more.

AC: So, you mean to say, as an actor, you have no boundaries in your head where you say, 'I cannot go beyond this point'?
RS: You know, once I decide to take the plunge, I decide to take this risk, and it is a huge risk.

AC: It is.
RS: Yeah, it is a lot about optics for mainstream leading men. In your real life too, you are pretty much perceived as the character you play on screen. So it was a massive risk for me. I am glad and relieved that it was worth taking the risk.

AC: Did you have to think about it? Or did you instantly say yes?
RS: Oh yeah, I was initially very apprehensive, and on various counts. When I first read the part, I knew I'd have to tap into some really dark places in order to play this character, and I wasn't ready to do it at that point, that stage in my life. I was in a happy space. Whatever darkness was within me I wanted it to…whatever had been brushed under the carpet, I wanted it to remain there. I wasn't ready. And so it took some convincing. Mr Bhansali really was insistent that I explore this part, and all credit goes to him. I'm glad he was able to convince me, because I was scared. I knew that I would have to go deep into the rabbit hole to explore this character, and I was petrified at the idea of it.

AC: You know, I had done an interview with Mr Bachchan right after *Ram Gopal Varma Ki Aag*, and he said to me that when you play a bad character, all of the bad stuff (the darkness swept under the carpet, like you mentioned) comes out, and it's actually like catharsis.

RS: Yes, he is absolutely right. I am fully in agreement with it. It's like taking the garbage out of your being, collecting it and then burning it. That combustion is the performance. I really had to confront my demons. I had to even revisit negative experiences of my life.

AC: What do you mean when you say you confronted your demons? Like how bad can Ranveer be?
RS: Or I have been...

AC: So you absolutely have to go there?
RS: I have to go there. To the places I don't want to revisit in my life, and that was really scary initially. But Mr Bachchan is right. You come out feeling lighter because you addressed all of your darkness. It is like Diwali cleaning of your aura. You know, once I come out of it, I become so much nicer, lighter, kinder to people. I had bottled up all that garbage inside me and now it's all gone.

AC: So you are a better man for having played this character?
RS: Yes, you could say that.

AC: You told me that when you guys were shooting *Bajirao Mastani*, it was terrifying, because you knew you would give it everything you have, and Sanjay would be eating popcorn at the back.
RS: (*laughing*) I was like...I am putting my heart and soul into this. I won't do it again.

AC: But you also said that when you got the character right and he was happy, he would come up to you and say, 'Areey! Mere Daniel (meaning Daniel Day-Lewis)!'

RS: He (Sanjay) is brutal. If you are not getting it right, he is going to let you know. But if you get it, he is so effusive in his praise that you feel like the king of the world. You have put everything into the character, and for that to be validated in that way in front of everybody...he really has a way with the actors. He is a very, very special director.

AC: So, tell me. In this movie, was there a scene when he came up to you and said, 'O mere Daniel'?
RS: In *Bajirao Mastani*, we worked in a very different manner. It was like I was doing my own work and he was reacting to it. This time, however, he was a part of the process from the word go. I was executing the way he told me to do, so it was different. I was drawing a lot more from him this time, because Khilji is one of his favourite characters. He has a lot of things he wants to do, and you have to live up to that. He was having fun with it. And we were having fun together. I think, out of all the films, this was the most fun I had with him.

AC: Really?
RS: Yeah, if I was Alauddin Khilji, then Mr Bhansali was my mirror. It was like he and I were both Alauddin Khilji at the same time. We were having a blast!

AC: Tell me what happens when there are three amazing actors in a movie and one gets all the attention. Does it make life difficult, or are you all so evolved that it really doesn't matter?
RS: Who got the attention?

AC: You!
RS: Okay, thank you for saying that! But I won't take it for granted.

AC: No, but does it make things awkward?
RS: Why would it? Everybody is part of the same film.

AC: So you are serving the bigger picture.
RS: I am not into one-upmanship at all. I have done a two-hero

film. I've done all sorts of films. I'm not into these competitions. I have a theatre background, so for me, it is all about collaboration. It's a very collaborative process. My foundations are built in collaboration and I know that you are only as good as your co-actors. Take Jim Sarbh, for instance. He makes me look good by what he does. He enhances my performance. Or with Alia Bhatt right now in *Gully Boy*. As we are telling you off-camera before we started this interview, I feel like I don't have to do anything. She is doing it for me. I just have to be there, react and be present with her. This is the type of collaborative approach I have towards my work. When we are learning acting, that's what we would do, right? All the actors would be part of the same warm-up exercise, and it's all collaborative. I'm not into doing my own thing and then obsessing about 'let's see what he's got'. I'm not into this competitive vibe at all. I find that it harms your creativity; it is rooted in negativity.

AC: Absolutely.
RS: From my point of view, I need to, as the leading man, be a leader on the set and make sure everybody is happy in this environment and working and thriving towards giving their best. And I want to be that way, and, in fact, towards everybody with the same sort of positivity.

AC: Ranveer, this film has had a very tough journey. How did you stay positive? I have thought a lot about it. What does it do to an artist? How did you keep going in spite of it all?
RS: I was not positive. In fact, I was very sensitive. I can't tell you the kind of fury I felt when that first incident happened. I had to be calmed down by the people around me. I was ready to go on a rampage. I mean, how dare they!

AC: Yes, absolutely.
RS: That is my place of worship. Don't come on a film set and do that. You know, assault somebody that I worship. I was full of

rage. But I decided that instead of acting out and being destructive about it, I would be constructive about it, and I channelled all that angst into my performance. That's the best I can do. Channel it, and make it work. Now the film is released and it is what it is. Everything that you see is born out of something, a cause. You can choose to channel it in a positive or negative way; it is up to you.

AC: Then, at what point, in the last few days, did you feel you were apprehensive about doing this role? Were you afraid of what would have gone down after this? At what point did you say, Okay, I'm through... I've passed the test?
RS: I don't look at myself and my performance in isolation. When I saw the film, I was viewing it as a film.

AC: Sure.
RA: And I was in tears and that was very fulfilling. Mr Bhansali's endeavour was to evoke a certain emotion out of the viewing audience, and he was successful. That is nothing less than a victory in my book.

AC: What was the hardest scene?
RS: You know, the hard part was the delays and other such issues. A lot of my portions came one after the other. Typically, in a costume drama, it is so exhausting mentally, physically and emotionally that you shoot six to eight days and you take a break because you need to recover in order to attack the next part. Unfortunately, I didn't have the option. We were running out of time, and my portions had not been shot, and a lot of them came back to back. For instance, I shot more than forty days in order to complete the film, which is unheard-of for a costume drama, especially on Mr Bhansali's set, where you have to do so much. I think it was on Day Thirty-seven that I thought my brain had become mush, my body had become pulp and I didn't know whether I was coming or going.

AC: Really?
RS: It was very, very difficult. The shooting process was very

difficult, the action scene was the final battle with Shahid, and that was extremely difficult. Shooting 'Khalibali' (the song) was tough. I could barely stand, and I had to do this dance. And as much as my mind wanted to, my body was giving up, my muscles had failed, and I couldn't stand. I had a hard time shooting because of the way it was being shot, but I don't blame anybody. These were just extenuating circumstances that pinned me against the wall. It was just the way it was, and so, I had to dig very deep in order to keep going, considering how physically, mentally, emotionally exhausted I was. Because of those delays, in the action bits which I had to shoot in May, I found myself under four layers of leather, just melting. My body was just melting. And there was such hardcore action in that kind of heat, with burning tyres, because you had to create that war atmosphere. It was a toxic environment to be shooting in, and then when they called 'cut', I would see stars and just collapse on the side, vomiting.

AC: Literally?
RS: Yeah, I found myself on my knees, vomiting plenty of times, and bleeding. So, it was a very, very difficult shooting process. But yes, when you see it, it's all worth it. Now, I am like...YES!

AC: I also love the scene where you are in a coma and then you kill your nephew on that bed. And you say...what was it?
RS: *Sultan banne ke liye dono, gardan aur irade, majboot hone chahiye* (To become a sovereign, you need to have a strong neck and a strong will).

AC: Yeah, such a killer line. How did you have to work on the sheer physicality?
RS: The Alauddin Khilji workout was eating a lot of red meat and lifting really heavy weights.

AC: That's the Khilji workout?
RS: It's very simple. I am actually very excited to share this. I ate red meat for a year and a half straight.

AC: Every day?

RS: Yes, I thought to myself, if I want to subscribe to the notion that you are what you eat, then I'm going to eat red meat throughout! So, yes, I had been on a diet of just meat. Just as that eating scene that you see was what I was eating for a year and a half. Just meat...gnaw...gnaw! And yes, it was a lot of fun. I personally like being a big brute with big muscles. The *Gully Boy* physicality, being lean, is not really my thing. So, it was a lot of red meat and a lot of heavy lifting.

AC: So, Ranveer, when you go through an experience which is physically and emotionally so draining and demanding, how do you...

RS: In the prep process, I found this image of a silverback gorilla and I said, 'That's it! That is Alauddin Khilji.' I had that put up, and used to constantly draw strength from it. So, I sort of like that facial expression, that physique, physicality—that's all it was, you know.

AC: But tell me, how do you leave a man like this behind?

RS: On the last day of shoot, boom! He is out. I couldn't wait.

AC: You were done with it?

RS: Yes. It was very much like *Bajirao Mastani*. *Bajirao Mastani* took some time because I died on screen. But this time, the minute I was done, bang! And it was gone! You know, I had to get it out. I was like leave, leave *(laughing)*... So, yes, the last day when we rejoiced and cut the cake, I went home and I was done.

AC: You know, Shah Rukh had said that he takes a shower to get rid of the character. Do you have any such rituals?

RS: Yes, I do. Some that I cannot share *(laughing)*. I think yes, it's a shower and then I have the night clothes that I wear, the stuff that I've owned for fifteen...eighteen years. The same T-shirt, same pyjamas, that kind of brings me back. When I get into that and chill on the couch, then I am kind of back, you know, I mean back home.

AC: Tell me, Ranveer, before this film, there was, of course, *Befikre* which we must address, since I am still being trolled for liking it as much as I did.

RS: 3.5 stars! Never forget.

AC: Absolutely (*laughing*). What did the failure of the film teach you as an actor?

RS: I am trying to assimilate what I learnt from the failure of *Befikre*. Let's see. I don't view it as a failure even if others do. I still got to collaborate with somebody special—Aditya Chopra. It was a very successful process for me. For me, the process is the prize. I always say this and I mean it. I don't know how people perceive it, I don't understand the box office numbers. All of that is not my concern.

AC: But doesn't it break your heart?

RS: No, it doesn't.

AC: You can walk away and be done with it?

RS: Like I said, for me, there is no greater gift than to be able to go to a film set and perform in the capacity of an actor. That itself is a prize, a gift for me. There I have accomplished what I set out to. For me, everything else—the good, bad and ugly—is either a bonus or not. For me, I already got my prize—the one dream I had of becoming a mainstream actor in Hindi films. I am even thankful for being able to go to a film set every day and do what I do. So the acceptance, the fate of the films, affects me very little.

Also, I have this sort of middle path approach. I don't get carried away with the success of a film or bogged down by its failure. If I sometimes do, it is very briefly, and then I move on to the next thing only because, again, that is the gift. The prize that I am on a film set, making a movie. That's the joy. I've got what I always wanted.

AC: It doesn't impact your choices at all?

RS: My choices are a function of what is being offered to me. You know, sometimes, like right now, I am in a very good phase. I have got *Gully Boy*, I have *Simmba*, and then I have '83 in the pipeline. So it is a solid time...touch wood!

AC: It's amazing!

RS: Sometimes, exciting films don't come my way for months on end... But I'm really thankful and blessed that I had this period where such wonderful films were offered to me and I'm doing them. So I am really, really happy. I am looking forward to my upcoming films.

AC: Tell me. What are your compulsions now as an actor? What do you really want to do?

RS: I really want to do these films—these films that I just mentioned. I'm damn excited about them. I was excited to do *Gully Boy* and I am in the thick of it, and I am thoroughly enjoying it. I try and be in the moment as much as possible. But if I have to think forward, then I am really excited about *Simmba* with Rohit Shetty. Then there's also '83, which is an incredible human interest story—an Indian story, and perhaps my biggest challenge yet. Somebody just asked me whether this movie (*Padmaavat*) has been the biggest challenge, but I can see another huge challenge coming up.

AC: Where you play Kapil Dev?

RS: Yeah, how are you going to get that speech pattern, that physicality and that bowling action right? You have to turn into the character. It's going to take some doing. So yeah, I'm salivating at the prospects that lie ahead of me. I'm really excited. So, okay, if I really want to do something in the future, it would be something in the English language.

AC: Really?

RS: Yes, I went to a school where the medium of instruction was English, and it is one of my main languages. I studied in the United States. So I really want to do something in my other language, which is English. There have been some opportunities that did not work out. I know that the right thing will happen at the right time and I really want to explore that. I think I'll be good!

AC: I am sure you will be good. Now, I think it's been about five to six years since I have been having these chats with you. I remember you coming on the sets of *The Front Row with Anupama Chopra*. Do you remember I had interviewed you way back, and then you rapped? I think it was right after *Band Baaja Baaraat*. I have seen you grow into this massive star.

RS: We've done some memorable interviews. Why am I not being able to recollect this particular instance?

AC: This was the solo one. This was way back, I think at least five years ago. You don't seem like a very different person to me now. You seem like the same guy who came there and rapped. How do you do it? How do you not let the surround sound around you, which is now deafening, get to you? For example, when you step out, do the fifty people taking pictures of what you are wearing affect you? How do you not let all of that go to your head?

RS: I am very blessed that all this is happening to me. But, I never lose sight of that one big thing that happened to me, right? Like I told you. The only thing I ever wanted to do, the only thing I ever wanted to be, was a Hindi film hero, and here I am, doing it. It's the greatest gift ever, and I am thankful every day for that. I don't lose sight of it.

AC: Or a Hindi film villain?
RS: (*laughing*) Well said! Well said! Done that too!

AC: Thank you so much, and just keep soaring. It is such a delight to see you on-screen and to talk to you.
RS: Thank you. Likewise!

The Pursuit of Beauty

Sanjay Leela Bhansali

I finally managed to get the reclusive filmmaker, Sanjay Leela Bhansali, to do an interview after pursuing him for ten months. I really enjoyed listening to him talk about his creative process, where his incredible music sense comes from, and why he's so elusive.

We also discussed the scars of his blockbuster, *Padmaavat*, starring Ranveer Singh, Deepika Padukone and Shahid Kapoor, a year after its release. He speaks about the trauma he underwent leading up to the film's release and why no filmmaker in the world should have to endure what he did.

AC: Tell me, Sanjay, why are you so elusive? It's almost been a year to the day *Padmaavat* was released. Last January (2018) it released and became a blockbuster and after that you just disappeared. What have you been doing since then?
SLB: Nothing. Getting over the trauma I went through. I think no filmmaker in the world has gone through or should ever go through what I went through. It was neither civil nor right in any

way. For a filmmaker to invest in something that is so ambitious and to do a film as difficult as *Padmaavat*, and then having to go through morchas of three hundred to four hundred women outside the studio, is not on. It is a relentless assault on the mind and the entire nervous system.

But, I was relentless and just went ahead and made the film my way. I did not allow any of these problems to show on the screen, guarded it outside the studio gates, went in and forgot about it. It takes a lot out of you to be able to put up a shot which is so beautiful...that I think is so beautiful, then realizing there are people shouting outside. It's not just about me, it's about the people working with me. To shoot a film with some fifty cops surrounding you, through Film City, through the three months. Or to be physically attacked. It was pointless, it was uncalled for. And then there was the stress about whether the film was going to be released. All that took its toll.

AC: Do you feel healed?
SLB: Absolutely. I felt healed the minute the people responded to the film and said that there was nothing to protest about.

AC: Exactly.
SLB: The kind of love for the film—$550 million worldwide, the biggest overseas—that calms you down. You also feel humbled because you care for your work so much. And I have lived with *Padmaavat* ever since I did *Padmavati*, the opera, in 2008. So, something I have lived for, nurtured in my mind, made it happen, eventually manifested into what I had imagined. I felt good about it in some ways. Healed, yes. I went completely quiet because that is the only way to fight it. I let my work speak for itself and to take the approval of people, besides the Censor Board, wasn't necessary. So this silence became a part of me, this past year, within which I was obviously thinking, writing and creating what I had to so that I can start my next film. But yes, it has changed my perspective, it has scarred me. It has changed me.

AC: In what way?

SLB: In lots of ways. How much to trust people, how much to get up and believe in the freedom of expression, whether I need to take the approval of twenty thousand people. That you are at the mercy of people who can just get up and say anything. It's a very scary thought. I was just short of being lynched, so at the end of it you wonder. These scars are not eventually going to disappear. But I am not letting them bog me down. I am in a very good space—a very calm, humbled, meditative space. It was a lesson to keep you grounded, rooted. I loved that film and it is one of my best works.

So, yes, this year has been quite introspective, assessing my flaws, looking deep into what I want to say after twenty-five years of making films. In 1994, when I did *1942: A Love Story* with Vidhu Vinod Chopra...from there to now it's been a long time. I've gone through *Khamoshi* and *Saawariya*, which were colossal failures, to *Padmaavat*, the biggest hit. I've seen it all...I've seen failure, I've seen love, hate. They've attacked my work, loved my work...all sorts of things. I've sometimes felt jealous of filmmakers who have made very good films. Loved some of them.

I am a complete human being in that sense. I've seen failure, success, love, hate, experienced anger, jealousy...everything. So it's a wonderful space to be in as a human being, to understand these emotions. It helps you as a filmmaker to understand and portray different characters. So it's been a year of turmoil, slowly, slowly coming down. It's easy for someone to say, 'Why don't you snap out of it?' It's not that simple, something that you can just snap out of.

AC: I don't think any of us can even imagine what that space must have been like. So let's get the rumours out of the way. Are you making a film with Shah Rukh and Salman?

SLB: (*laughing*) You, yourself, are saying 'rumours'. If it's a rumour, why are you asking?

AC: You have to say yes or no...

SLB: (*smiling*) These are rumours. I don't need to sit and answer rumours, and justify them.

AC: I feel like you are. You are side-stepping it. And you don't lie very well, so you're smiling as well.

SLB: I don't have to accept all your feelings, and all that you feel about my films, my future projects. It's about my feelings, and what I want to do. No, I have not yet zeroed in on the film I want to make from the three subjects that are very dear to me.

AC: Can you tell us anything about any of them?
SLB: In the next interview!

AC: Which will be ten months from now?
SLB: (*smiling*) Ten months from now, and ten months after you pursue it!

AC: (*laughing*) Okay, so here is what I was thinking when I considered the films you have made. Even when the films are based in contemporary times, like *Khamoshi* or *Goliyon Ki Raasleela Ram-Leela*, they are set very much in a Sanjay Leela Bhansali world. Of course, you decide the way the characters speak, the way they dress, and they are not connected with a reality that is outside this office. So, I have to ask, do you have a God complex? Like Gaitonde says in *Sacred Games*, 'Kabhi kabhi lagta hai ki apun bhi Bhagwan hai (Sometimes, I feel I too am God).'

SLB: Not at all. It's just that I create my own world. Every filmmaker does it. Raj Kapoor did, so did Satyajit Ray and V. Shantaram. That is the filmmaker's state of mind, his understanding and perspective of life and how characters should behave, and how they should look. I look at it differently from most of the directors in the industry because I am who I am, and they are who they are. So, despite the fact that you may not relate to them in today's times and feel they may be from a different time and space, I am still in love with my characters.

AC: Of course, there is an emotional reality.

SLB: I think that's my style. It's the texturing of my frame or the kind of 'textiling' I use, the kind of art and colour I use; all that comes in. For me, a film is bringing the five or six art forms together, whether it's music—classical or Bollywood, architecture, painting or textiles. Whether it's the dance forms, or all its art forms, I don't think other filmmakers do it. I have my own understanding of the frame—and within that frame all these art forms come together. I can't ask a painter why the Mother Teresa he has painted doesn't look like the real Mother Teresa. But I get a sense of Mother Teresa being painted.

AC: It's what it evokes?

SLB: I have my own style of filmmaking. And I think a lot of people like my filmmaking because they find something different in it. But, primarily, it is my way of interpreting life in my own warped sense.

AC: You know, when you did a few interviews around *Padmaavat*, you said, 'I'm dying to get back into the studio because the cinematic part of my brain is peaking.' Does that mean you find more inspiration, does it mean you have more clarity as an artist? What does it mean when you say that the 'cinematic part is peaking'?

SLB: I feel, right now, I need to talk less. One of the main reasons is that I express myself more effortlessly, and with more control through a visual, a scene, a sequence or a film. I don't find the need to talk in words. So, when I go to a studio or a floor (when I say studio, I am talking about the floor), I get fascinated. It is my absolute temple; it is my place of worship. Whenever I enter an empty floor, I get goosebumps.

AC: Really? Even now?

SLB: Even now, even after suffering for this one year, for not being able to start a film because I wanted to calm down and get my energies right. I am writing relentlessly every day...so that I can go to the floor and then transform it into my own world and say, 'Okay, fine, there was nothing; it is bare walls, it's a catwalk.' I think I've always said that my Gods live on the catwalk, I don't need to look any further into the heavens and say, 'God help me.' I feel very inspired, I don't know if I have told you this, but I was, as a four-year-old child, taken for a shooting by my father.

AC: Yeah, you told me.

SLB: And I was fascinated by the world he put me in, a cabaret shot. I knew this was my world. And his words were very clear, 'Don't move from here, don't go away from here.' And I still feel the essence and the power of those words, because I just want to keep going to that world...that is my world. My world is not my office, it's not the roads, it's not a holiday; it's just the four dark walls. And from there to imagine sounds, to imagine songs, to imagine art transforming it into a world that you seem slightly uncomfortable with.

AC: (*laughs*) We will discuss this after.

SLB: Yeah, but I feel that I am now enjoying filmmaking far more effortlessly than I did ten years ago.

AC: The strain is less?

SLB: No, in terms of how to construct a shot, how to improvise.

AC: It comes easier?

SLB: It comes easier. There was a time I could not convert whatever was on my mind because of my inability to communicate with so many people. I talk more effortlessly on the floor now and I get what I want. It's been happening since *Goliyon Ki Raasleela Ram-Leela*, and I am far more in control of the form, so I just want to keep living. That's my life, I don't live any other. I don't go for dinners; I don't go for movies. I've been to two movies in the last two years.

AC: You don't watch movies? You're not interested?

SLB: I don't go to the theatre and watch. I am consumed by the thought of just the film that I want to make. Even now if I want to go for a drive, I go up to Film City and return home because of the joy of going on that road and all those...Sunni Maidan, my *Ram-Leela* set, my *Bajirao* set. The nostalgia is an important part of wanting to say, to be inspired. A lot of people find it a little difficult, and say, 'But you don't go out, you don't...' I am enjoying the world and the space that I'm living in.

AC: And you savour your own company?

SLB: Completely, because you're constantly thinking, you're constantly living in some other world. I cannot connect with people around me. I'm like, 'Yeah, are you done?' Because my mind is saying, 'Aha, something has come to my mind.' It's not normal or healthy for a lot of people because they feel that you are overdoing it, and you need to be a little more relaxed. But I enjoy every minute of pursuing it to the point of madness...to the point of almost punishing myself...to the point of saying that I have no sense of guilt that I give it all, as far as filmmaking is concerned. And outside of filmmaking I give nothing. So that's the way I am.

AC: (*laughs*) But Sanjay, that doesn't mean that you are not interested in people?

SLB: Of course; I'm interested in people, I like people.

AC: You have to. Right?

SLB: I love people, I connect; once I meet people, I'm just always worried about how this person will react. Will he say this? I have my own screenplays because I am constantly writing screenplays, so I start writing screenplays about people.

AC: So you have a whole fiction in your head?

SLB: So, before I enter any place, there is a whole screenplay in my head, which is completely fictitious, nonsense, it is not necessary, but once I meet people I am charmed by, I am charming enough to charm them and we all have a great time. I am very accessible in that sense; you can tell me anything, I am a great listener; I will listen to your criticism. I have listened to it over the years!

AC: Yeah, you have.

SLB: And I have appreciated you for speaking, leaving the friendship aside. You've said what you wanted to say. For those five minutes, I'll say, 'You know, Anupama has gone mad,' when I am reading it.

But she has the right to say what she wants to say. I appreciate that, so I'm a good listener (if not a good talker), I enjoy people a lot. But then again, I get consumed by what I want to do. A lot of people don't agree with my kind of films but I have found a large audience that I meet on the road when I'm travelling, or when I walk to get my cigarette, or when I'm travelling with my window down and smoking. People are just constantly saying, 'Wonderful, we like you.' I say, 'But how do you know me?' I hardly come on television, I hardly go anywhere, but that connect with the work is so immense that I feel it's worth staying in that meditative state and realizing that it really pays off. It's a state where I am consumed, so now when you ask me a question, it becomes difficult for me to snap out of something and say, yeah Anu, let me concentrate, because I have to be true to this moment and say, 'Yeah, let me talk about what you have to say.'

AC: Correct.

SLB: But I've started living, I think, for a lot of people, in La La Land.

AC: Alternate reality (*laughs*). You know, Sanjay, I watched *Padmaavat* again for this interview, and I was again just struck by how beautiful the film is. You know, just the beauty that you have in each frame, it's perfect, down to sort of how much her chunni will slip, or one tendril of hair will come out like this.

Where does this hunger for beauty come from?
SLB: From the lack of beauty that existed in my growing years, in my formative years. We lived in a very poor house. We had no paint on the walls. Mom was a wonderful dancer, so she would dance in that small hundred by hundred flat when the radio would play a song she liked. We didn't have good clothes to wear. So there were a lot of things that I felt deprived of as a child, but my mind was always a filmmaker's mind. Whenever I would do my homework, with Mom teaching me, I would be looking at the wall and wondering what colour it should be.

So my mind was preoccupied with finding beauty in that lack of beauty in my life, or lack of space. Therefore my sets are humongous. I feel deprivation is a very important part of a true artist to find expression. It's only when you crave for it and only when you call for it from deep inside your soul and you see that one little line that Latabai sang in that one song, it's etched in your soul and you wonder where her music came from. It came from a lot of angst that singers today don't go through. I want to find beauty, beauty not in the sense of plastic beauty and snow-capped mountains and daffodils and flowers.

AC: Sure.
SLB: That's not beauty for me. I find beauty in that little thread that comes out of a shawl a weaver has woven. It's hours and hours of work with the costume designer, with the art director, painting and repainting, and to be able to block it, and to be able to get the character right and then forget about all that and concentrate on the narrative and on the scene. It's a lot of effort. Once I'm there, I'm not there even for myself. I sometimes wear torn pyjamas, and my assistant says, 'Sir, your pyjamas are torn.' I say, 'Bunk it, let it be, let's just concentrate on the work.' My buttons are not there. Nothing matters.

What matters is how I create that one moment of beauty within which I also tell my story, and it also says something about the character. How those characters feel. Half the time my job is done with the actors because they wear a certain outfit, made in a certain way, put in a certain ambience, and are given a few lines. And they immediately respond to the colour, the weave, the texture and the background music I play on the set for them to emote. It's just not pursuing beauty. For me, it's a frame.

AC: It's a texture?
SLB: It's something that I'm constantly pursuing, to frame as sacrosanct. A lot of filmmakers do. It's great to see a lot of slice-of-life films that are being made, and they run into the lanes with handle cameras; that's also beautiful. But the frame has to be correct, so I'm constantly pursuing that. I feel really guilty if I feel a shot is not right; I come back and reshoot, I redo it. I can't live with something that is not done to the best of my ability. Somebody can do it better, I'm sure, but I need to pursue it.

AC: But you've always, Sanjay, had this eye for beauty. Did you cultivate it, or was it just there?
SLB: No, it was there. I was constantly being told to watch V. Shantaram's work, and Raj Kapoor's work, and Satyajit Ray's work. My father was a film producer. He did not fulfil his dreams; all his unfulfilled dreams became my angst and therefore I kept going back to what he was saying, what he was trying to pursue, who these filmmakers are that he's talking about, why he is constantly playing the Lata Mangeshkar song for me, and Bade Ghulam Ali Khan, and Pandit Aamir Khan Sahab, and Gangu Bai Hangal, and at the same time playing Dada Kondke for me and saying that is also important. But I think that comes naturally. You cannot cultivate it, you cannot say, '*Gaitonde Sahab, aap aise paint karo* (Gaitonde Sir, please paint like this).'

AC: It's in your DNA.
SLB: It's there. You're born with it. Then you're born in a place which is deprived of all beauty, then you pursue it, find it, and you

find your mission, and you find your expression. It could be, people say, I am three hundred years old, as a soul (*laughs*). Sometimes people see a piece of song and they say we get gooseflesh. What is it that creates the gooseflesh? It just cannot happen; it comes out of so many years of accumulative ability to say, okay, finally that moment culminates in the frame or that moment or a song that I shot, but it comes from many, many years of living it, craving for it, knowing it; somewhere in the subconscious it has stayed, so it's a very complex thing, but it's a great way of finding your expression and being there.

AC: Sanjay, you just said the frame is sacrosanct. That's something that you really live by. You also said, I remember in some interview, that when you are on your deathbed and you're watching your films, you don't want to see a mistake in a frame, and have to live with that. Right?
SLB: I've decided there are two films which I will not see in my life, when I'm going.

Those two films, don't bring them in front of me, because they are mistakes. Yeah.

AC: (*laughs*) Which ones?
SLB: That secret goes with me.

AC: But tell me, when you are constructing down to the last detail, does it leave enough room for spontaneity or imperfection that actually lets you breathe a little?
SLB: Everything is spontaneous, all the homework that I do as a filmmaker of knowing a scene and understanding it, everything is changed on the set.

AC: Meaning you have one idea and then you get there and you change it all.
SLB: I rehearse it one night with the actors, then I come in the morning and I change everything. So the actors, Ranveer, Deepika or Priyanka, after a point, stopped rehearsing the scenes

the previous night. They said, 'One second, Sir, you're going to change everything in the morning.'

My improvising and spontaneously reacting to the scene is what makes a very deep impression on people when they watch it, and there is a power that generates from it because it is not studied. That perfection, which you find and mix with spontaneity, that's the whole challenge which I've overcome over the years and I've found my way to be spontaneous through finding perfection. So once I've improvised, I want it to play, then I sit and change the colour or the costume and do all sorts of things. By the time I take my first shot, the actors have a nice nap, they come back, so it's constant writing with the camera on the set.

I was shooting this bathtub song in *Padmaavat*, with Jim Sarbh, and Ranveer was in the bathtub. I didn't know what to do. I went over there and said, 'Jim Morrison and Zeenat Aman, mix the two in the tub.'

AC: No! That was your brief? Jim Morrison and Zeenat Aman?
SLB: So Ranveer said, 'Give me one hour, I need to first debrief myself; I don't understand what the hell you're talking about.' And when he came, I said, 'I don't want to see a rehearsal; we'll go for a take straightaway.' He didn't know what hit him, and when he performed, I was so moved by what he did because that is how an actor is improvising. We had no brief, we didn't know what to do, and it's constantly discovering the moment on the set.

AC: But did you think of Jim Morrison the night before? Or did that come to you right then?
SLB: As I was driving.

AC: Oh, as you were driving?
SLB: As I keep listening, suddenly I change something, then I'll say, 'let's do this', then suddenly I'll say, 'let's do that', so it's constantly living that moment. Once the space comes alive, once the characters come there, once you know everything is in place,

then you respond very differently from what you've planned. Even after the rehearsal in the morning, after we've changed everything, I still change things when they come back. So they come, and the first thing they say is, 'Hope there are no changes, because we've ratto-ed (memorized) it in our minds.'

AC: And then you say, 'No, there is yet another.'
SLB: 'Can we do it tomorrow?' And I'm graceful enough to understand that it derails them. 'Okay, we won't do it today, we'll do it tomorrow.' Because that moment is very precious, so if it means a little extra money, it doesn't matter, extra time, it doesn't matter. Let's live it, and live it honestly. That honesty within finding spontaneity and perfection is very expensive, it's very time-consuming. I took two hundred and sixty days to shoot *Padmaavat* because that's how I make my film.

AC: And the producers?
SLB: They don't ask questions.

AC: That's a great privileged position to be.
SLB: And I won't answer if they ask me any questions, so that's how it is.

AC: Do you let them come on the sets?
SLB: Yes, sometimes they do come on the sets. I'm not very comfortable, but I'm not uncomfortable either. It's their money they are putting in, it's their privilege, and they are very kind to me, they've been very cooperative with me. Viacom was very wonderful throughout the making of *Padmaavat*, through all the problems we went through, to stand by, and to pursue it and not give up, and say, 'Let's shoot it.' They are wonderful people. Ajit (Andhare, COO) had great vision to be able to put so much money on a film that on paper seemed like it would never recover.

When you believe in something, and you believe in a director... I mean, what more respect can I ask for from a studio head who believes and says, 'Okay, I'm with you. Let's just go and do what you want to do.' I am blessed, so I feel that all that I was deprived of as a child, in terms of not being able to get a paint brush on my wall, God has blessed me with all that. I can paint as much as I want to. So it's a lot of hard work and prayers and wanting to... Somewhere that energy also questions your passion and your belief in what you want to do, and then it gives everything to you.

AC: *Chhappar phadke* (in abundance).
SLB: Yes, *chhappar phadke*.

AC: You know, Ranveer told me that of all the three films he's done with you, *Padmaavat* was the most enjoyable. He said, 'I became Khilji, and my mirror was Mr Bhansali. We were both Khilji.' So I want to ask you, Sanjay, how much of these characters come from you and how much of residue do they leave behind?
SLB: Oh, completely. I dived into the evil side of me and the dark side of me, I exorcised the demons in me completely. I said, 'Do this, do that.' Every time Ranveer would walk in, I would say, 'Come in, come in, and sit here.' He would say, 'This scene, Sir, I have memorized...' and I would say, 'No, leave it, get onto the bed. Now take the crown and push it into her face.' So I would start doing all these things. And he would say, 'But, Sir, are you all right?' I said, 'No, no, do it, I mean it.' Then I would say, 'Push her on the bed and all your hair on to her, like a snake moving over her.'

AC: Right.
SLB: He would say, 'Sir, are you really a good human being? You've got to be an evil human being.' I said, 'Just do it, I'm enjoying the dark side of it.' You are not a complete person if you don't accept your dark side. We all have a dark side and a good side and a bleak side. As a filmmaker, as I keep saying that all my bitterness, anger, jealousy, love, laughter, humour, everything has to be brought on a platter to be able to see. If you are a 'very good filmmaker' who speaks good lines and is very well behaved, always laughing

at the right time, then you're not expressing yourself fully as a filmmaker. You must be hated, you must understand hate, and you must understand love.

AC: Right. *Sab ras* (all the flavours).
SLB: *Saare ras ko samjho. Fear hona chahiye aapke andar. Woh fear ko aap kaise express karoge, aapke character ka ek fearsome situation hai.* (Understand all the flavours. There has to be a kind of fear inside you. You have to know how to express that fear. Your character is in a fearsome situation.)

AC: Right.
SLB: So if you've not experienced all this, you don't express it when the time comes. With Khilji, I was having a blast. With Ram, in *Ram-Leela* and with Leela also I had a blast, because she was a little whacked out, and I enjoy doing mad characters. A lot of people feel I'm a very serious person, I talk very little, I'm inaccessible, enigmatic. I'm nothing of this sort. I'm a very happy person. Yes, I'm quiet. I am intense. I can skip into the dark side within a fraction of a second and you won't know who that person is, but when I'm enjoying life, I'm enjoying it to the fullest through my characters, not through my own personal living. I save it all to live through my characters, through my films that I want to do, so there are riots in *Ram-Leela* that I've shot and there are action sequences, and a gun in the hand, and all that I would never do in my real life. I save it for the screen.

AC: But in life, Sanjay, you don't want to actually yourself live some of this?
SLB: Of course, I'm living it. I'm living the life I've chosen. I'm enjoying everything. I've always waited to do this. At the age of four, I decided that the little cabaret that I was seeing being shot was what I wanted to shoot all my life. *Woh forbidden apple jo kha kha ke phek rahi thi woh cabaret artist, woh forbidden fruit maine kha liya tha us din* (The forbidden apple that the cabaret

dancer threw after chewing, I ate that forbidden fruit that day). I want to live only this. I am enjoying it and I just hope that I have more energy to do a lot more work, because my mind is exploding with so many ideas in so many ways to do a thing. I'm just ready to go to a floor and shoot three films at a time, I feel right now.

AC: You know, one of my favourite moments in *Padmaavat* was when he puts the perfume on the girl and then rubs her against himself (*laughs*).
SLB: That was my subconscious, it was on the set. I said, 'You know, just splash it on her.' Ranveer said, 'Yeah, then?' I said, 'Now pull her and rub her against yourself, so that you get the fragrance.' He said, 'Sir, are you mad?'

AC: It was amazing, because it captured who he is, so completely.
SLB: Yes, but it also captures who I am completely. It also captures the anger in me, the arrogance in me. I'm letting it all out, and experiencing, what you call, the cathartic side.

AC: Yeah, cathartic side.
SLB: Just purge, purge all…because you need to evolve as a human being. I've changed a lot from what I was ten years ago as a person, the way I respond to situations, to everything. I've become far nicer, and in another ten years, the plan is to become even nicer.

AC: Really?
SLB: And to become even better as a human being because I feel nicer and you keep purging, there's a lot to purge, so I'll take another ten films to cleanse myself. But I think it's a process. You evolve as a filmmaker, as a human being, enjoy life in your own way, finally find God somewhere waiting for you there, and he says, 'Well done.'
When I say God, it could be…

AC: Anyone.

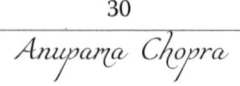

SLB: It could be Raj Kapoor, Shantaram waiting there to say...

AC: At the pearly gates... (*laughs*)

SLB: 'You did well, you did well.'

AC: (*laughs*) Such a great visual, that is such a visual. They'll pat you on the back (*laughs*).

SLB: Sometimes I feel they come and are hovering around.

AC: Really?

SLB: You have to invoke energies. As a filmmaker, it's a world of illusion you create, and if you connect to illusions in the right sense, in fine poetry within that illusion, even if it's telling a simple scene of two people arguing over a mundane, stupid, trivial thing, you still give it a certain dignity. I suddenly get up and say, 'Do this,' and then I come back and say, 'But that's very Raj Kapoor-ish. Where did that come from?'

AC: Really?

SLB: And then I start wondering, and I go back and sit in the edit and say, 'This is like Mehboob Khan shooting Nimmi.' So I am, of course, enamoured by those people, K. Asif, Kamal Amrohi, all these great filmmakers. We don't make films like they made anymore. We are too much into edgy, raw, and then they get great reviews and you all say, 'Oh it's a great piece of work because it reflects life in society.' Did none of Shantaram ji's work or Bimal Roy's work reflect life or society? Some of them did, a lot of them did.

AC: Yeah.

SLB: A lot of them did but when they had the need to do... *Mother India* was a great social statement also, a great work of art.

AC: Yeah, absolutely.

SLB: When you come to *Navrang*, which I love immensely, or *Pinjra*, these are where Shantaram ji is tripping as a filmmaker.

AC: Correct. There are no boundaries.

SLB: He has a right to. And today we write off these kind of films and say, 'Oh, but that's a legacy.' That is what a legacy is all about. The West went completely mad watching *Padmaavat* because they said, 'Ah, finally we see the exotic, old lyrical India; we've understood a part of where they lived, the way they had kind of...' That whole evolution of a nation from where it is to where it was.

AC: Sure.

SLB: So it's important to also talk about those things and everything doesn't have to be raw, edgy and real. It can touch a social cord, an issue.

AC: Yeah.

SLB: They are very important films. I am not looking down upon them.

AC: Yeah, but you need all kinds.

SLB: All kinds, but this kind is normally looked at with great skepticism now. 'Oh, he's spent so much money, so much time. Look at the luxuries afforded; look at this, oh look at that. Why should these be looked into? Do you also look into the kind of trouble and problem and the angst and pain that I go through to make it? No. So, look at this side, of what God has allowed me to afford today. So I go through it, and so has Kamal Amrohi, making ten years of *Pakeezah*, or ten years of *Mughal-e-Azam*. They are cult films. We are still deriving from them.

AC: Absolutely.

SLB: I'm still very jealous of K. Asif sahab and I feel, when will I ever be able to make a film of that calibre and that nuance and lyricism of being completely connected to the supreme? Kamal Amrohi was connected to another energy, another level of creative angels. When those creative angels are invoked, they stand by it for ten-twelve years, and nothing changes, nothing goes away.

Look at these great men. Where are these great films being made? I feel I'm the only one left over here.

Of course, there are 18 historicals being made, but with these kind of invoking creative angels, you could call any soul that you know. Deep down, you say, 'Suddenly she looks like Waheeda Rehman walking in from '*Waqt ne kiya kya haseen sitam*' (What beautiful agony time has given). How is it happening? Because somewhere I am invoking those energies all the time, praying to them, talking to them, looking at the work, worshipping them. So, *Bimal Roy se leke sab* (from Bimal Roy to everyone)... So, there is still so much to explore as a filmmaker. I better get down to making films fast, rather than trying to get out of the trauma of *Padmaavat*.

AC: No, no, listen, that's done, and it was a huge success. But tell me, Sanjay, I want to understand how you work. You have a very long-standing relationship with your writer Prakash. What is the process? He is writing, sending it to you? Do you do so at a certain hour of the day?

SLB: Very random. When the moment comes, it comes. It could come while having coffee here, it could come when I am talking on the set, improvising, suddenly we meet, we talk, we discuss this, this, this and this. Now, look at *Devdas* between the lines, from what Sarat Chandra has written. I don't want those lines, but I think there is something in between we can discover in the idea of Paro and Chandramukhi meeting. So he said, 'Blasphemy!' I said, 'Doesn't matter,' but in Bimal Roy's film they crossed.

AC: They crossed in the train, right?
SLB: In the palki.

AC: In the palki, right, she was walking by.
SLB: But that was not in the text. It was not in the book, so if he has improvised...

AC: ...you take it further!

SLB: Yes, I take it further and with time you explore it. There are going to be ten more Devdases being made in the next fifteen years. This is a story that will live in the minds of Indian filmmakers. They'll always want to tell that story that we found and improvised, and suddenly he will write the scene and come—and he writes random scenes. We will start with writing scene number forty-eight.

AC: No!

SLB: And that's how the forty-eighth scene will come to me. I say, it's fabulous, I am moved, I've gone mad reading that scene and then suddenly scene number five will come.

AC: But how do you connect the dots?

SLB: But I'm so used to it, and I also live with it. One line is read and I'm also working. Then I send him five lines.
I think, then suddenly I'll send him two ideas. *Prakash bhai, aise kiya toh* (How about doing it this way, Prakash bhai)? So it's a lot of give and take, and I really respect that man's writing. He is a genius.

AC: Where is he based? Is he in Mumbai?

SLB: We lived in the old chawl which I keep talking about, where I lived my childhood. He was five buildings away.

AC: Really?

SLB: Living in a chawl there, we were also relatives, because he is also a Bhansali, but we never met for the twenty-eight years of my life that I lived over there. I had never seen Prakash bhai, because I would be in my home; I was a recluse. I was an intense and introverted child, as was he. We met for Devdas and he said, 'I lived in Madhobag.' And I said, 'I lived there.' Then he said, 'Oh, you were in that place?' Can you imagine? We didn't know, we had not seen each other, but what a writer, what a genius in his own right.

AC: So, it's just a back and forth?

SLB: Yeah, it's those abstract ideas that he can put together. Then I take his writing a notch up and I say, 'Okay, you wrote a great scene, but I am going to shoot a better scene than that,' so we have our own challenges among ourselves. And he says, '*Accha, dikha do, dikha do, dekhte hain hum bhi, kya karte hain* (Okay, show me, show me. Let me also see what you do).' It was constantly trying to take each other into searching for excellence by challenging each other. But my filmmaking is very random; I never go to an outside location or a great place to write a screenplay. I want it to be my office, as chaotic as my office is always, with five thousand things, and then I'll say '*Yeh saaf nahin kiya, yeh theek nahin kiya* (You have not cleaned this, you have not corrected this)'; all that is constantly going on. Why I would come on time? So I'm occupied with all these things.

AC: Housekeeping and writing.

SLB: In office as well as here. You've come five minutes late. Why are you five minutes late? It's like I create chaos around me to be able to find that one thought that says, 'Aha, I solved it; I've found something.' Now that chaos is irrelevant. I was with Vidhu Vinod Chopra for eight years. I learned so much from him. I saw his eccentricities; he was full on.

AC: Yeah, yeah.

SLB: And I took everything from him and then I realized I should not have taken that long because I had picked up...

AC: *Kuchh cheezey nahi learn karni chahiye thi* (You should not have learnt certain things).

SLB: *Nahi learn karni chahiye thi, woh bhi seekh lee* (I have learnt even the things I shouldn't have).

AC: Vikram Motwane, who assisted you, talks about what a great education it was for him.

SLB: You have to express fully. I think if a flower blossoms

35

completely, there are thorns also that come with it, so you have to express yourself as a living entity to your fullest. Some things are acceptable, others will hurt; some things will have fragrance, and then you will perish at the end of it, so while it is blossoming and while it is growing, you must do it to your fullest.

AC: Bloom away...
SLB: Bloom away. Otherwise, you are leaving so much unsaid within you. You say no to impropriety, and show only good behaviour, what will people say? Sometimes, when I have evolved into a better human being, people still say things about me, so they are not going to stop saying things about me. They will still call me...

AC: *Kuchh to log kahenge* (People will say things, let them).
SLB: *Kahenge* (Yes, they will). They still call me arrogant, they still call me obnoxious. I am nothing of that sort. I am a very simple person. My favourite city is Film City, my favourite food is daal chaawal, my favourite pastime is watching the news, and that's it. And I just live, and make. Do you know when I made Devdas, I had a small one-bedroom house and I used to live in the hall. Mom used to be in the bedroom.

AC: Yari Road?
SLB: Yari Road. You've been there?

AC: Haan, I've been there.
SLB: And Rekha ji came one day after Devdas, and she was a little surprised, and said, 'You live in this house?' I said, yeah.

It didn't strike me that I didn't have a bedroom. It didn't strike me, it didn't matter...nothing mattered. It was only that we had music sittings, and costume meetings, and art meetings. *Devdas* was a humongous film at that time.

AC: I remember that set was unbelievable.
SLB: Now, those things (*he trails off*)... But the director didn't

have his own bedroom. When you come from the night shift and you find the maid *jhadoo maroing* (brooming) in the morning right next to your face at 9:30, you live with all that. Therefore, I am a grounded, down-to-earth person who is arrogant about the fact that I lived what I lived.

AC: How do you create music? You have no formal training. I was trying to figure out who else? I think apart from Vishal Bhardwaj, you are the only director-composer with no formal training. How do you create something as magical as 'Lal ishq'?
SLB: In the bathroom, under the shower.

AC: Nahi (No)...you're standing in the bathroom and 'Lal ishq' comes to you?
SLB: Yeah I just sang 'Lal Ishq'. It was written, so I lived with it, and then I was taking a bath one day, suddenly I started singing. So, a song does not have to come like I take my instrument, sit at a piano, take out my harmonium and a tanpura, and then say, let us create a song. A song can never come like that. I've listened to so much music, I don't live without music. If I'm writing, there is music. If I'm bathing, there's music. My music plays non-stop, twenty-four seven in my house till I switch off the lights, and sleep. It's non-stop.

AC: Okay.
SLB: I've heard so much music that I respond musically to a lyric, to a line, and I've made songs as a child. When I was a child, I was not very interactive. Sitting alone on a terrace in that crowded Bhuleshwar area, I would sing a song. My escape. I would take the lyrics of...I used to go and buy film books. There used to be film leaflets.

AC: *Haan, haan* (Yes, yes), booklet types.
SLB: I used to go and buy them for twenty-five paise or whatever it cost and I would remake the song. So, with *'Chura liya hai tumne jo dil ko'*, I went and remade *Yaadon ki Baaraat*, and I made my

own '*Chura liya hai tumne jo dil ko*'. I was a little 'off' as a child, a little demented. My father and mother were sometimes worried when they heard me sing my own 'Chura liya hai'. They would say, 'Are you sane, are you there? Will we need to take you for some treatment?' I would make my own songs. After *Saawariya*, when I was rediscovering myself after that box office 'bonanza' or whatever I went through, I said, 'Let me look into all sorts of areas of myself that I have still not tapped into.' So I took a song and sang it. I'd sit in my farmhouse alone on a swing and sing. Then I would record it on my phone with great difficulty. So many of them. I've lost very nice songs because I pressed the wrong button or deleted something or whatever.

AC: But they don't stay in your head?
SLB: They stay if I sing them again and again and again. Then I come here, and I have a music team, and I say, 'Here's a song.' Sometimes they add to it, sometimes they correct it; we all do. I think music, film, everything is something everybody contributes to. I cannot say I am a filmmaker and I do everything. My costume designers add so much more to that brief, and make it their own. So everybody together makes a film. It's not like writing a poem, or it's not like a person painting, or a person drawing an architectural plan for a building. It's great collaborative work.

AC: But it just comes?
SLB: It just comes. If I don't let it simmer and live longer, it goes. I've really sometimes hurt myself about a lot of songs which I thought were very good, but have disappeared. I'm constantly singing and making songs. Some of my favourite music composers are Jaidev ji and R.D. Burman, and all those greats.

AC: That's amazing. What a gift!
SLB: Yeah it is. It's getting better and better for sure. 'Ghoomar' was so difficult to create. 'Binte dil' was so difficult. I've created it out of nowhere and now there are versions being made in the

Middle East by singers and very big stars. I don't know if you have seen them.

AC: Right.

SLB: So it's a great moment of pride for me to realize that their biggest artistes are singing a version of 'Binte dil'.
I don't know Sa, and Re, and Ga, and Ma, and Pa. It's just spontaneous expression.

AC: Amazing.

SLB: Are we done?

AC: No, we are not done! Now, with the benefit of a year, away from *Padmaavat*, you have the benefit of hindsight. You know, when I watched it again, that last scene is so powerful, and it's so beautiful, that sea of red and those women and those flames. Do you, when you sit down to create that beauty, think at all about the messaging? I mean, now, when you look back, do you think there is any merit in the argument?

SLB: Chittor bleeding at that moment was the sea of red. You are talking of a beautiful visual because it was shot beautifully, laid beautifully. Overnight I made a well. I said suddenly this jauhar cannot work if they don't go down the steps.

AC: Right.

SLB: So, over one month, while we were shooting on this side of Sunni Maidan, they were making that jauhar set. For me, it was the whole power of running into a fire, which is against all human logic and possibility because no human being can run into a fire. And these women had decided, 'We are going to run into a fire.' You don't even get an iota or even a shadow to see. It is gruesome.

AC: Is it glorification? Do you see any merit in that argument now when you look back?

SLB: Of course, that is the way it should have been. There was no other end to the women in Chittorgarh at that point of time, and there is no other alternate end today. If I want to tell the story again I would say, 'The women...at that point everything was over, they had to win the war,' and the war was about surrendering. They didn't surrender, they ran into the fire. It is not glorification to say all the women were helpless and they didn't know what to do and, therefore, they were pushed into the fire, and oh it's gruesome. No, it was an act of war, it was an act of courage. Hara-kiri was a part of the time when women had to do it because the kings lost the battles. They had to surrender and go through the humiliation of being put into the harem, and go through all that, or die with dignity.

AC: The doors are closed.

SLB: She fought, the king went to war, and he lost. When finally the siege is about to happen, there is no choice, and what a brave act. Why did I want to make that film? The courage to be able to find your power at that point of time, what is right at that point of time. It may not be right today for a woman to run into a fire in case of adversity or for what she is facing. You fight back. However, after all that, there could be a time when you realize that there is no fightback, so either you give up or you fight. But now you need to take a stand, and there is no glorification or beautification of it.

They were women in red; they wear red when they wear red. I did not design it to make it look beautiful. I didn't want to make it look gruesome, and I saw them going into the fire because that could have been extremely gruesome to watch. It is not possible. I would not have been able to see it, but that is why I made this film, to salute the power that these women generated when they went. Chittor bled, and that red that was floating through the steps. It was, for me, the high point of my filmmaking. Not a word in the climax.

AC: It was a stunning sequence.

SLB: It was fifteen minutes of just silence. It was just music and it was just people finding their own way of how to fight that moment and win at any cost. And win they did.

AC: But do you think at all about the messaging when you were creating it?

SLB: No, not at all. What messaging? I am telling the story that happened, that the message was courage, and finding your strength. I'm not a documentary filmmaker; but I love watching documentaries. I understand they are great revelations in understanding human suffering and whatever is happening in the world, but my cinema is not about social messages. It's about a work of art, working on your mind to make you think, and say, 'Do we subject women to this?' 'Should a woman go through this?' 'Do women do this en masse?' What is happening the world over where women are being subjected to all kinds of torture, unheard-of and unacceptable things? That is what my work should provoke.

If it makes you think whether it was right, or wrong, that is an achievement for me. And a work of art should make you think, it stimulates some energies in you, which it does. A good painting does; so any work of art that sets your senses tingling, and therefore makes you think that, is also a purpose of art. When Hussain paints something, what social message does he give you? When Taj Mahal was made, what social message did it give? When a great poet talks of personal angst, not of socially relevant poetry, but when he writes poetry of romance, what social message does he give? Does art necessarily have to be a social message?

AC: Not at all.

SLB: Lata Mangeshkar has then done no social service for that matter, but for me she is the most important human being in the industry because she gave us art of a level which is unheard of. We cannot even imagine that kind of excellence in pursuit. So she is the greatest, but she is an artist, which has got no social relevance. Yes, there is filmmaking, there is poetry, there is every kind of thing that also questions and addresses, but pure art, when it sets your emotions, makes you cry, makes you smile, makes you think, makes you want to create it, to live it. These are also purposes of art.

AC: Yeah, and what next, Sanjay? I know you said there are three projects and you won't tell me anything about any of them, but how soon do you get back into a studio?
SLB: This month. I shall announce this month and then get into the studio.

AC: Wow!
SLB: So I'm raring to go.

AC: How exciting! Cannot wait to see what you do next.
SLB: Yes. Are you done?

AC: (*laughs*) Done. Sanjay, thank you so much.
SLB: Thank you.

AC: And I'll never be really done. I could ask you questions for at least another half an hour.
SLB: Thank you so much.

Fearless Women

Anushka Sharma

Celebrating actor-producer Anushka Sharma's seven years in the industry, we sat down for a conversation where she talks about life as an actor and producer and the difficulties and irritants that come with it.

Anushka opened up about the issues that plague the Hindi film industry, the latent as well as blatant sexism, not just when it comes to remuneration but also in terms of the quality of roles. She also spoke about her now husband Virat Kohli and how they maintain a sense of normalcy in their lives.

AC: Anushka, this interview is for you to celebrate seven years in Hindi cinema.
AS: Ooh...so cheers to that!

AC: Since you and I both don't drink...it's apple juice.
AS: Children, don't drink. This is what we do in films also, right? When we are shown drinking champagne, we are actually drinking apple juice.

AC: But you don't drink at all?
AS: Not at all.

AC: Never ever?
AS: I have, but then, I just stopped one day. I used to wake up in the morning and…just didn't feel good. So I thought just for those few hours I don't want to go through a full day of downers. So I just stopped.

AC: So, apple juice it is.
AS: And I don't think I need to. You've met me, Anupama. I have so much energy. I think maybe I need to take something else to calm me down. In fact, I get very happy at parties when people drink, because I think they're finally coming up to my level and I can behave the way I want them to!

AC: I can be me!
AS: Exactly!

AC: Everyone's drunk now.
AS: And it's amazing, when everyone drinks at parties and comes and tells you things and you're listening to everything. Drunk people want to tell you things, and it's like you have a superpower!

AC: Listen, it's been seven years, but what a year it's been! Amazing! First, you kick it off with the biggest blockbuster ever, and then in January you follow it up with *NH10*. I don't know the numbers, and I've just been told it's a ₹13-crore film with adult certification that made ₹35 crore in India. That's pretty damn amazing, girl! Was that in the real sense like, 'Yes! I did it!'?
AS: It definitely was a real sense of achievement and probably the biggest achievement I felt, because while I was very fortunate to be launched in a very big way, the film that got me the most recognition and success was *Band Baaja Baaraat*. So it made me feel really good because I felt like I could take more pride in this because there was a new director, a new actor, and people

liked me. It was like being able to do something that was bigger than yourself because when you're making a film like *NH10*, you know it's not going to make that kind of money, because, firstly, it's a film with adult certification and secondly, it's not a very... you were getting scared while watching the film and you were terrified of it...

AC: I shut my eyes in parts of the film...
AS: There were people saying it's a fantastic film, but if you get scared easily, don't watch the film. So, it's a hard-hitting film and not conventional in that way. But you did it because you believed in that film, the story and the people who were behind it. And I think, somewhere, to be able to create something...that's the first time it happened for me.

AC: There's an extra satisfaction, isn't it?
AS: It's an amazing feeling, because at the end of the day we get paid a lot of money, we are successful, famous and all of that. But somewhere, I felt like I had done something, because I have never been someone who has chased money. I'm not someone who has ever chased fame. So this, to me, was personally a very satisfying feeling.

AC: Anushka, this is what happens a lot in the West. Somebody like Reese Witherspoon will buy the rights of a book and then make a film because that's how she controls her own persona. For you, is it a way of doing that? You control the material; you control your career in a far greater way.
AS: I don't think it's controlled, because one thing I have experienced is that things are not entirely in your control...

AC: Even as a producer?
AS: Because you don't have the money, right? So, the control is in the hands of people who have the money. What we have is creative control, which is what we want. As an actor also, I've always been very vocal about things. Right! Whoever the director

might be, I have always said what I... If I have a suggestion to make, if I have a point to make, I've always said it, and sometimes they've listened to me and sometimes they haven't. That's because you're just trying to, in that case, just give your best, right?

Here I would say it's about actually being able to create something, being able to bring people together who have different points of view, who are telling a story which is unique, and to be able to put all that together. I think that is something that you have control over. After that, it's just, it's a lot of *magajmaari* (a lot of tiring work), such as pitching films back and forth, about things being spoken about the budget, and *yahan pe kaato*, and *vahan pe kaato* (cut this and that down), and it's just about *kaato, kaato, kaato* (cut, cut, cut) and you're just like, '*Please banane do, please banane do, please banane do* (Please let me make it, please let me make it, please let me make it).'

So, right now, we are in a place in the industry where we have these corporates who are there in the studios, big studios which are here. What also happens is that when the really big, big films don't do well, and a lot of money has been put in those films, like one of my own films this year, *Bombay Velvet*, then it is very difficult to push smaller films. Because then people don't want to. I am not saying that those small films are always risky, but sometimes they are, and sometimes you want to take that risk.

NH10 was that risk, but sometimes even that much they don't want to do. So, being able to do that becomes difficult, and that's why I say there is no control. There is creative control, of course, but even then I am not doing it, because I just want to control everything. We are working on three films right now.

AC: Three films as a producer?
AS: We are developing three scripts right now. Two have already been developed, so you let the writer write. We trust them; we know what they're doing, and you can jam with them. It's a creative

process, just like what two musicians would do. That's very, very fulfilling. I was telling my brother yesterday that I had a meeting with a writer and we were just discussing some things, some concepts, and I felt the happiest doing this. And when I'm acting. Everything else that happens sometimes is too taxing for me as a person, but these things are what really get me going. The ability to be able to do that, I think that is very rewarding, and I feel very grateful for that.

AC: But it is also, Anushka, shifting the needle when you become the producer. It also shifts the needle a little bit for women in Hindi films. This year, in 2015, this conversation on women and films has really reached a critical momentum, especially in the West. So, *The New York Times* recently did this huge article about what the state of women in their industry is, and just listen to the statistics. It's amazing. Okay! In both 2013 and 2014, only 1.9 per cent of the directors for the 100 top grossing films were women. Excluding art house divisions, major studios have released only three films last year directed by a female director, between all studios. In 2014, 95 per cent of the cinematographers, 89 per cent of screenwriters, 82 per cent of editors, 77 per cent of producers in Hollywood were men. Think about that...and this is an industry we consider...

AS: As progressed...

AC: *Progressed, bade evolve ho gaye hain woh log* (they are very evolved). They are ahead of us. For India, we don't have these figures but the Gina Davis Institute on Gender and Media Studies actually reported that Indian films, and not only Hindi films, have a significantly higher prevalence of sexualization of female characters. They are at absolute bottom as far as female speaking characters are concerned. They show female characters in less than one quarter of all speaking roles.

AS: Yes, yes.

AC: I mean the numbers just hit you.

AS: Yes. I might not know the statistics, but this is absolutely true, and I experienced it. This thing that you are talking about, speaking roles...

AC: Yeah, yeah.

AS: Girls are just expected to be like good-looking, and just be interesting enough for a guy to fall in love with you in a film, right? Women, who we've spoken about, women doing films together, they only come together in a film if there is a boy involved, like if it's a love triangle or something like that. I think, firstly, in India, I would say it is also reflective of a society. That's the way we want to look at women, and one huge example of this is that men can work as long as they want to, even if they've aged. It's fine, they are still heroes, and they are still superheroes, and they are still amazing and cool and all of that, which is fine, and I have no problem with that. But why is it that women are only okay till they are young, desirable? So, to think about it, desirable means what, like there is a sexual connotation attached to this, so we're actually looking at women in that way in films.

AC: Only?

AS: Only, and we are looking at women that way in films because we have only shown mostly that to people in films, barring a few. So till that does not change, right? I'm not saying objectification of women, even if you're not showing tits and ass. I am not saying that, but just what you are bringing to the film. Other than your beauty and your nakhra (coquetry), is there anything else you are bringing to the film? Till that doesn't change, we are going to be in this situation. So, although this year has been really good for women because a lot of films that have done well have actually been films with female protagonists, I think this is also happening in our industry now because actors are backing these kinds of films.

AC: The men?
AS: Actors, actresses, both.

AC: For both?
AS: Yeah.

AC: And the fact that you are a producer means there is a change.
AS: No, but look at this Anupama; you're in the business. You know for a fact that even when actors produce films, they get a huge amount of money and then there is a percentage, and all of that. But with actresses, it's really not like that. We have to literally say, okay, I'll produce the film, so that the film can be made in that much of a budget, otherwise this film cannot be made. Right?

AC: Right!
AS: So, I mean you always feel that discrimination. In fact, it's not just with money, it's also in general. I swear to god, even if you're in an outdoor schedule, you know that the guy is going to get a better room than you.

AC: No!
AS: Yes!

AC: Are you serious?
AS: Yes. So I think, why does that need to happen? I'm sure every hotel has two really good rooms, right? But, if there is a better option among the rooms...

AC: So it's even on that level?
AS: Yes, and you see it all the time. You see that, it's there. You know what, when I was growing up, my parents treated my brother and me with absolute equality. I did not even know the difference. I didn't know I was a girl. I might not like to do a lot of boy stuff.

AC: Right, matlab the physical stuff.
AS: Yeah, I would play sports and stuff, but I was not treated

differently. I never felt I was lesser or I was discriminated against. I only experienced it after I became an actor, so think of that. Fine, I was very young when I became an actor, I was nineteen, but dheere dheere (slowly) with my experiences in the industry I started to see that difference, and it happens. It's a mindset thing. We talk about how, in our small towns, women are treated, are discriminated against, and it happens even here. And it is very apparent. I mean, you can't be shocked about it, Anupama. You know that...

AC: No, but different hotel rooms? I mean, that too, for me, is shocking.

AS: Yeah, of course. I mean if there is an option of giving an actor a better room, you would give an actor a better room, it is the way it is. That's how it is, and these kinds of things are like, yaar, come on!

AC: Yeah, it's just...

AS: Yeah, but then it's done because that's just the way it is in our society. The boys are more important. It's just there. Let me be very honest about it.

AC: It's just there.

AS: It's there. For example, even if there is an actor who is probably at the same stature as me, he would probably on his own, not without an actress, be able to bring only that much money for a film, but would still get paid more than me because he is a guy. It's just there, but nobody is even thinking about it.

AC: All else being equal, he will still make more money.

AS: And you know what, it's not like they are thinking, oh I'm going to treat this one lesser... It's just there, Anupama.

AC: Ingrained?

AS: Yeah, it's ingrained. So, no one is going out of their way to do that. It's just there. That's how it is.

AC: But that's so sad.

AS: And today, we are talking about it, we are speaking about it. For a long time, people did not talk about it. I know for a fact that a few years ago when people were being asked this question, they were saying no, it's not like that, and being diplomatic about it. Today we are talking about it because in all walks of life, women are earning money and the power game has shifted. It's not the same, so that's why I guess today we are even speaking about it. Honestly, I am saying this again and again that it's not like we go out of the way to do it, it's just there.

AC: It's a natural thing to do.

AS: It's a natural thing. That's how you're thinking, that's how you've been. And I swear to God, it's even evolved. People in our industry, the big names, and sometimes some other people tell me, 'Oh no! You're like an activist.' So I was like, 'I'm an activist? Like why am I an activist?' Because you're saying all these kinds of things...

AC: So that makes you an activist?

AS: It makes you an activist. People don't like women with guts in this industry. Yes, I'm a very young person saying these kinds of things. I was twenty-five when I'd decided to back *NH10* as a producer, but that is actually my dream. I want to be able to leave some films behind me, not just as an actor, but as a producer, which have actually shifted things in the industry.

AC: Just move the needle, right?

AS: And it gives me happiness to do that because I feel like it's a cause bigger than myself. But when you're only thinking about yourself, I can do that, Anupama. Do you think I'm not in a position where I can just do the big films and just be amazingly gorgeous and just be that way? You think I can't do that? Of course I can, but I don't want to because, firstly, it does not give me satisfaction as a person, and secondly, you can call me an idealist. It is a bit

---

In Conversation with the Stars

selfish, like we can kind of contribute. Like MAMI, it's a film festival where we are seeing all kinds of films. This is a change, right? Because people are able to, and I know so many of my writer friends, who had tickets every day because they wanted to go in to catch those films. That is changing our setup. That is changing our industry because now we have a festival. So, if it becomes really, really, really huge, it's a country where we make so many films. We make so, so many films. We have to have a successful festival, right?

AC: That's what I feel.
AS: Exactly. So, what I am saying is, we need to do these kinds of things to change. That's the way I look at it. And I am not saying I want to change things because I am some kind of, *kya bolte hain usko* (what do you call it)?

AC: Activist.
AS: Yeah, activist, exactly. I'm not an activist. This is what I want to do. But it's not looked at in a way that it's like...

AC: ...not positive?
AS: Somehow it's seen as 'bada ban rahi hai (she is trying to be too big for her shoes)'.

AC: You're speaking too much.
AS: Yeah, 'bahut bol rahi hai (she is speaking too much)'. That's how it's looked at. And honestly, I'll tell you something, in our society you've never seen a girl picking up a freaking rod and hitting these goons, these horrible, horrible men. You've not seen that kind of a film, right? So when in theatres people were clapping at that moment, and not like our screenings...

AC: The real theatre.
AS: The real theatre. When I saw it with my own eyes, I was so overwhelmed. I'll tell you why, not because people are clapping at my film, sure, that also, but also because I was thinking that they

are accepting a woman doing this. Like you usually see heroes, men doing these kinds of boys' stuff, right? But when you see a woman doing that, that itself means there's a change.

AC: Some things have shifted?
AS: So, now if we know that people want change, I'm just taking a risk. No, people want change and that's proof enough. Now why can't we push it? Someone asked me recently, 'What is the one thing that you'd like to change?' And I was reminded of this thing that I told my friend. I said, 'You know what, we are all so lucky that we live in India because the taste here is so mediocre that we all are "stars"' (*laughs*). So we should be very lucky that the taste of people is very mediocre, right? So we are all stars. So, we all should know that.

AC: But that's amazingly incredibly kind of self-aware of you...
AS: It is a fact, it is that. We are not really pushing ourselves that much, we're not getting enough opportunities.

AC: You are not killing yourselves.
AS: If tomorrow I want to go for these workshops for a film... so what is Anushka doing? Anushka is doing a workshop? Why does she need to? These kinds of stupid, cheap things which kind of mean nothing...those kinds of things.

AC: You are trying to do too much method?
AS: Yeah, meaning it's literally like that. If I ask too many questions to a director, he's like, '*Oh ho mera sar kha rahi hai ab yeh* (she is eating my head).' It's like that, right? When you are asking too many questions also, that's the way it's looked at. Because it's okay, *jo hai, jo ban gaya hai, voh theek hai, itna is enough* (whatever has been made so far is enough).

AC: It's okay to be happy.
AS: But think about it. The only reason I know there can be a change or we can push things is because there have been some

people who have done it. Someone asked me something and I said, you know I just want to be like Nawazuddin, and they were like, he's a guy. I said, yeah, so? I want to be like him!

AC: Yeah, look at his performances.
AS: Look at his performances. I just want to be like that. So all of us need to have that.

AC: You need to be hungrier.
AS: You need to be hungrier. People are hungry, but hungry for...

AC: Success.
AS: *Jahan pe jo mil raha hai* (wherever they can get it). Like I was talking to Kalki and she did *Margarita with a Straw*. And she was talking about how that scene, the nude scene that she did, it was an eye-opener because she felt that a disabled person is never looked at in a very sexual way.

AC: Not at all.
AS: Like they are asexual.

AC: Yeah, that's the last thing you think of.
AS: Exactly. But by doing a film like that, what has she done? She has put a thought in someone's head.

AC: Kangana had said this. We just had a conversation at the Mumbai Film Festival about women in films, and there was Kangana and Vidya and Shabana and Ava DuVernay who was on the jury, and Kangana said, 'I have experienced that when I have suggested things, like you were talking about suggestions, people don't understand, and think she is such a bitch.' She said it's just like that.
AS: Yeah, if you are asking for something that you think you deserve, you are a bitch. She has attitude. *Isko kitna attitude hai* (she has so much attitude). You are not being unreasonable. Listen, we are not stupid, we are not dumb, we've come so far in our life, not by being stupid and by being like a floozy.

AC: Yeah, yeah.

AS: I would say that all the actresses right now in the industry, you know, they have a mind, they speak, they are intelligent. I'd love to have a conversation with all of them, so if they are like that then obviously they are not unreasonable. If they are making a suggestion or if they are asking for something, they are being difficult. A female newcomer and a male newcomer will get paid different money. They will get paid different money; they will not get paid the same money. You're a newcomer, nobody knows who you are, man or woman, it doesn't matter. What you are going to get paid is not the same. It's just assumed that men need more money. Why? I guess, maybe people think men need to run a family, and that's why they need more money.

AC: And women don't, they are looked after?

AS: Women don't, we are looked after. I think that's the thing, *tumhare liye itna hi bahut hai* (this much is enough for you) because you're being looked after. Maybe I don't want to get married, maybe I want to get married, doesn't matter.

AC: It's irrelevant.

AS: Exactly, it's the value that I'm talking about. I'm not saying give me more money. Listen, I'm very blessed. God's given me a lot, so I am not saying out of greed *ki mujhe aur paisa chahiye* (that I need more money). I'm saying, just value me. At the end of the day you want respect. You want just that much. That's what you actually want. And when you pay me less money, you're basically telling me that you're not...

AC: You're not as valuable.

AS: You're not as valuable. An actress is doing a film on her own. Like, which actor is doing a film without a known actress or a hot actress? When I say hot, I mean like...

AC: Desirable.

AS: Desirable actress, or even like not desirable but just an actress who is known by people. Right! If I'm doing a film, in which my role might be a bit more than a guy's, I know for a fact that none of the guys are going to do that film.

AC: They won't.

AS: They won't do it even if it might be a great role. It might be, *'Lekin yaar, voh nahi hai us mein, balance nahi hai* (But it doesn't have that, that balance).'

AC: When Gravity had come out, I had put this question to at least a few men.

AS: George Clooney?

AC: I said, who would be George Clooney in this country?

AS: I'm so glad you did.

AC: No one.

AS: Nobody would be George Clooney. And how powerful that role was! Think about it, if you are working from a place where it's some kind of prejudice that you have in your head, or some preconceived notion. George Clooney did that film because he had the foresight to be able to see the potential of this role, because the role was...

AC: It's a critical one.

AS: Don't you feel you want him to come back? You want to believe that that guy was actually him. And for that you need a George Clooney. Imagine if it was in India and you'll have to take some other actor, then that film is not what it is. So I wish that people did that, but we know for a fact that they are not going to do it.

AC: Will other younger guys be any different? Sort of Ranbir, Ranveer, the next generation? You know, Arjun, Varun, you think their attitudes will be different?

AS: I think they'll be different till they do something which we'll see as different. How can we say if they are different or not different?

Let's see if they do something like that, then we will be, like, oh fine, this guy is different, he's doing something differently.

AC: *Because abhi tak to kisi ne nahi kiya* (they haven't done it till now).

AS: Yeah, they are all good at their jobs, they all do really well. It's amazing to work with them. They are nice guys and everything, but let's see if someone does it. I'll be like...for example, remember we had that discussion with Varun on the show, and I was really amazed. I was like, 'Good for you, man, that you did this film.' Like really good for you, but you remember what he also said, that there is so much pressure for this 100-crore business on actors that they get scared to take risks. So let's change that also. You understand the problem, right? The problem is not just that they're being so mean to us.

AC: It's at many levels.

AS: Yes, the problem is that there is so much pressure put on them also to make a 100-crore film. If a girl makes a 100-crore film, 'Arrey, she's made a 100-crore film!' It's a surprise. For men, it's like they have to make, you have to make a 100-crore film.

AC: *Ye toh hai hee, ye toh hai hee* (That is true).

AS: So, that 100 crore, I think you guys in the media, you all need to kind of really wipe this thing off the surface of this industry.

AC: Now it's gone to 300. Uff!

AS: Because it needs to stop, right? The film has done well, you can just give a figure, but to use that as a benchmark for success, that is corrupting the system—that is really, really corrupting the system.

AS: I think so.

AS: And that's why maybe people say that it is easier for girls to take risks because no one is expecting anything of them anyway, right? What are you expecting of them? So they're taking risks.

In Conversation with the Stars

AC: Because right now at least, it is the women taking far bigger risks.

AS: They are taking far bigger risks. That's true, they are.

AC: Yeah! All of you, I mean Deepika, Kangana, all of you guys are the ones who are doing the roles that are slightly more edgy, that are putting yourselves out. And the guys just frankly are not.

AS: Yeah, maybe. I mean, I'm really happy that Shah Rukh is doing *Fan*.

AC: Absolutely.

AS: It looks different and I know what the film is about because Maneesh (Sharma) is a friend. So I was amazed, and I told him. I said, 'It's great that you're doing this.' It is, because I actually want to see Shah Rukh like that.

He should be like doing a *Breaking Bad* kind of thing! That's how I'd like to see him.

AC: But Anushka, how do you stay sorted when you're at the centre of these kinds of ridiculous storms. When you're at the centre of the storm where, it's like okay, I've had something done to my face for a role, therefore, there will be a storm.

AS: Yeah.

AC: 'I was at a cricket match; therefore it will be a storm.' I mean, what do you tell yourself at that point? To just ignore the noise and say, 'just keep your eyes on the path that you're on'?

AS: I tell myself that if I start to listen to these people and start to let them decide how I should behave and what I should do, then this is not my life, it's theirs. They're controlling my life. I'm not going to give anybody the power to control my life, right? And I'm not saying I'm sorted all the time. It's difficult.

AC: Does it hurt?

AS: Yeah, I feel hurt sometimes. I feel insecure, I feel like, you know, *kya bolte hai usey* (what do you call it), being targeted

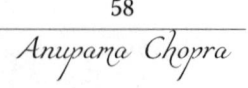

sometimes. But you know you have to just tell yourself that the option is, either you listen to all of this and don't go for a cricket match because people are going to say these things about you, or you do what's right. I mean, I'm in a relationship with Virat and he wants me to come to watch him and I want to watch him. Why the hell am I going to listen to anybody else? I'm not going to, because I know what they think is not the reason why things happen, right? So, if I stop doing that, then I'm actually believing what they're saying.

AC: Right.

AS: When I don't believe it, then it doesn't bother me.

AC: You are subscribing to it.

AS: I'm subscribing to it, so that's why it does not bother me. When people told me, 'Oh, so brave of Anushka to accept that you know she had a lip thing done' and all of that, and I was thinking like, I didn't think it was brave, you know. I thought it was normal. I don't want to live a lie. I don't want to be like, 'Oh, but actually it hasn't happened.' I don't like leading my life like that. I like to just keep things sorted in the sense that, just keep it real, and then your life is easy. This industry anyway is very difficult. It's a very difficult place to be in because there are all kinds of people and you're always going to meet ideologies and opinions and you know such treatment which is very, you know, not nice, so you have to rely on yourself.

AC: But isn't it hard, Anushka, because both you and Virat are in careers that are, first of all, extreme? You said somewhere that it's like, I have until the next hit on a Friday, and for him, it's until the next hundred. And you're playing out these extreme careers in public view. So you repeatedly say that it's been normal, and the sense of normalcy is very important to be in. How do you keep that sense of normalcy when you know it's always up or down, it's very extreme?

AS: In my relationship?

AC: Yeah, in a relationship, how do you keep the sense of normalcy?

AS: Because even he likes the sense of normalcy.

AC: So you both work towards it?

AS: We are actually the same people, except that I don't have so much aggression (*laughs*).

AC: Thank God for that.

AS: He's emotionally that way. I'm a little bit more emotionally like, you know, not get...

AC: Chilled out.

AS: Yeah, chilled out, but other than that we are exactly the same people. We want the same things from life and I think that's why we are in a relationship, and touchwood, in a relationship that I would say is normal because we both want the same things. We both don't want to become pawns, you know. Your life will go on, your life will go on, I am not going to start leading my life according to you. I've screwed my life up, so we both have a sense of that, so tomorrow... It is hard. It is hard for me to stand in a stadium if Virat doesn't do well, and you know, I feel as if I have done something wrong.

AC: And you know the camera is on you?

AS: I know the camera is on me but I'm great in front of the camera, so it's fine, that's okay, that's life sorted. But you know that these people are thinking you are the reason for it. Initially when that happens and you have to direct your thoughts the other way, you have to tell yourself that you need to be aware of that and both of us are aware of it.

AC: You really need to be tough?

AS: So even with him, we are very normal that way because we want normal things from life and we want to have a sense of, you know, reality, like both of us have come from very similar backgrounds. We both come from regular middle class families. Without any help from anybody in our respective industries we have reached where we are in our lives. So, firstly, there is a lot of respect for each other, and you know we are still those people. So, it's like our families are also like that, which is a very good thing.

AC: Which is essential.

AS: Like my parents don't want to be interviewed or come in front of the public eye. They have no interest in that because they feel uncomfortable. I'm not saying it's bad, I'm just saying they feel uncomfortable doing it.

AC: Thank you, this has been such a wonderful chat, and more power to you!
AS: Thank you so much. Thank you.

AC: Thank you.
AS: Cheers to that, man!

AC: Yes, cheers, more cheers!

The Radical Royal

Saif Ali Khan

From the dancing hero in the early 1990s, who, by his own admission, didn't know what he was doing, to the gritty cop Sartaj Singh in *Sacred Games*, it's been a rocky but eventful ride for Saif Ali Khan.

In the last twenty-five years, the actor has had the most interesting and inconsistent career with its fair share of lows as well as highs like *Dil Chahta Hai*, *Hum Tum* and *Cocktail*. The actor takes the viewers through the various phases of his career—the uncomfortable 90s, making his peace with the dancing, and slowly finding his stride.

◎

AC: Saif, welcome to *FC Unfiltered*. We talked about this for a while.
SAK: I know, because I saw your show and it was so watchable and interesting. I think I saw an episode with Sushant (Singh Rajput)?

AC: Yeah.
SAK: I called you.

AC: Yes.

SAK: And it was so interactive and nice that I thought it would be nice to come.

AC: It is, and we're so happy to have you here. You have, Saif, had the most interesting and inconsistent career. So I want to begin by just taking you through a clip and a couple of images, and I want you to tell me what your most enduring memory of that phase is.

SAK: Okay.

AC: Okay, so let's go to the first.

SAK: Oh bloody hell!

[The screen shows the song 'Main Hoon Aashik Aawara', featuring Saif Ali Khan and Mamta Kulkarni, from the film *Aashik Aawara*, 1993.]

SAK: Oh no! I have so many memories.

AC: Tell.

SAK: Saroj Khan choreographing and Umesh Mehra directing. Mamta Kulkarni was taking these white pills, and I said, what are you taking, and she said, 'They stop me from sweating.' So I said, 'But is it good to not sweat?'

There were no air conditioners in those days. We're in, I think, Natraj Studios. I think it's shut down now. I don't think anyone stays there.

AC: Yeah, haan (yes).

SAK: I was dancing on my knees later, and they were bleeding, and Saroj Khan was saying filmy things like, '*Dekho yeh khoon tumhein kahan pahuchata hai.* (Wait and see where this blood takes you.)'

I told her I won't be able to walk when I'm older.

That was that. It was really, really hot and I was having a tough time doing these steps. When it aired, it was a hit song. Akshay Kumar called me, laughing. He was just laughing non-stop on the phone.

AC: He just said hello and started laughing?
SAK: He said, 'Ha-ha-ha! What are you doing? Look at you.' He called it a masterpiece. He said, 'Bro, this is a masterpiece.' So we still laugh about this. I spoke to him recently about something, and he brought this song up.

AC: And how did you, Saif, at that time just say to yourself that this is normal?
SAK: Saroj ji said, 'Keep moving your hair.'

AC: So you were just doing it?
SAK: Yeah, it looks good, and I signed a couple of shampoo advertisements for Clinic All Clear and a couple of other brands.

AC: So it worked out well?
SAK: Yeah it worked out well. This was what, 1992? It was quite a cool haircut for then. I think I have the same haircut now. Oh no!

AC: Yeah. Time for an existential crisis.
SAK: Yes, full circle. Sorry, you were saying.

AC: Photo no. 2. This is *Dil Chahta Hai*.
[Saif is bare-chested, and wearing a bandana.]
SAK: Yes, this is *Dil Chahta Hai*. I don't think Farhan (Akhtar) wanted me to wear the bandana. I remember he told me, 'You're the only member of the star cast who looks like he's actually been on a beach before.' Because the rest were with umbrellas, looking very conscious of various things. We were shooting a volleyball sequence, I remember. We had such a good time making this movie. Those guys really know India and Goa and any kind of...I mean, the music scene or whatever world they get into, they really know it well. Zoya and Farhan both. So, it was brilliant going to Goa with them and eating in amazing restaurants. Suzanne (Caplan Merwanji), our production designer, had a beautiful home

with candles all over it and it was a very special experience off the set as well, making this movie. This was just another day at Anjuna beach or something, just working, and then rushing home to change and going out for another lovely dinner somewhere. Those were good days.

AC: So, Saif, when you were doing this, did you have any sense that this was going to change things?

SAK: There were a couple of things that happened, I remember. Aamir (Khan) asked, 'What else are you doing?' I told him the couple of movies I was doing. He said, 'This is a bigger film than both of those combined, so you have to do this.' So when Farhan offered it to me he looked really comfortable. I mean, he had a buzz cut, and he was wearing shorts and he was really trendily dressed and he came over with this script and said he wanted to make a film with sync sound and change the way films are made and perceived. I don't know if he was going out of his way to also change the way heroes are perceived, but there was something really new about it, but I was a bit skeptical because you hear some good ideas that don't end up looking as nearly as good as promised, so I was getting a little nervous. I said, 'Look, if Aamir Khan says yes, then I'm on.' Farhan still holds that against me. He said, 'How could you say that...if you liked the role and if you trusted me?'

AC: You should have said yes.

SAK: So I said, 'Well, I really respect his mind, and if he's just done *Lagaan* and if this kind of thing is okay with him, then it's okay with me. I'll let him decide.' And I did. Yeah. So that's that.

AC: That's that. Okay, photo no. 3. We go to this, in 2004 [a long-haired and clean-shaven Saif].
SAK: This is *Hum Tum*.

AC: Yeah.
SAK: This is a song. I had just finished doing *Kal Ho Naa Ho*. I

was working very closely with Shah Rukh Khan and I kind of got an idea of when the main lead has to do a little extra.

AC: Which is what?

SAK: Which is, I think, to be supportive of production, and your general demeanour and aura and idea and just your whole energy has to shoulder the production.

AC: So, not on-screen, but off-screen?

SAK: I mean on-screen and off-screen. I mean, somewhere, when you come to the set, you come with responsibility. The whole cast and crew were looking at Shah Rukh to carry this movie, and he would do it, and sometimes there'd be trouble, problems, production issues, and I saw him sorting those things out, and there was a lot of responsibility in his approach to shooting. Whereas in *Dil Chahta Hai* and these other roles where there were other senior stars on set, I left it to them and just basically had a good time. We were having dinner after the shot, but the main lead has to worry about a few other things also, so it was interesting that after doing *Kal Ho Naa Ho*, I felt ready. I was getting a lot of film reviews also, saying, 'He's good, but he's always good with somebody else. He hasn't had that breakthrough solo film', and Adi Chopra, I think, called Karan Johar and said, 'What's his role like in *Kal Ho Naa Ho*?' And he said, 'He's great and he's doing really well.' So he said okay. He said, 'I want to try and reinvent a multiplex hero; I want something new.' And this was that, and it was a really interesting film for its time. It's a really bad wig again, because we weren't very good at making wigs.

AC: I was just going to ask, what's going on there?

SAK: Because we had to have six different looks, from twenty to thirty-five, in the movie, and we weren't very good at making wigs, or they weren't sitting on my head very well, and there's a wire there and it kept rising and going up in different directions. We were trying to copy Tom Cruise's haircut from *Mission: Impossible 2* and there was a line in the movie too... I said, 'This is my Tom Cruise look' to Rani (Mukerji). I think I just made up that line, and the director liked it. So this was me getting a bit more comfortable, I think, with films and acting and being myself.

AC: And being the leading man?

SAK: Yeah, or there being a market for a leading man with this kind of energy, which was not the case when we were doing that first song.

AC: Next one.

SAK: Actually we weren't sure what the energy was when we were doing that first song.

AC: You're just like—we hope there is an energy.

SAK: Yeah, and what is that jacket? At the same time, I remember wearing an Armani jacket that I bought myself. I remember Katrina Kaif did that in *Race*. She had bought this slinky blue dress and every time she moved, the tassels would fly up. It was really a very hot number.

AC: The 'Zara zara touch me, touch me' song.

SAK: Yeah. She bought that herself and came to the set.

She said, 'I'm going to wear this.' Sometimes a little extra is needed. I should have taken off the jacket and said...

AC: The Armani?

SAK: No, the Armani was for *Yeh Dillagi*, the 'Ole ole' jacket.

AC: Yes.

SAK: This is much nicer than the green one. You can see the kind of thing going around in those days. The fashion was...

AC: A bit dodgy!

SAK: Yeah. I remember Aamir Khan again.

I told him, 'They're giving me these horrible clothes to wear. What do I do?' And he said, 'Listen, you can never say that you don't like the clothes because you don't want to come across as that person. What you say is that this is unlucky for you.'

He said that they'll run a mile, they'll burn it. You say, 'I love this green thing but waistcoats are very unlucky for me. Luck is a very big thing.'

AC: It is, it is, and who can control that? If it's your waistcoat, we'll get rid of it. So, did you ever use that line?
SAK: Yes, yes.

AC: You've done it?
SAK: Uh, well, only, only in one or two movies in the 90s, but I think I have done it. When all else failed and someone insisted I have to wear something nasty, I said once or twice, 'The truth is, this is really unlucky for me.'

AC: That's fab. Okay, moving on to the next one, which is also part of this, the multiplex hero.
[A scene from *Cocktail*, with Deepika Padukone and Diana Penty.]
SAK: Oh God! This is a bit fat with short hair. Yeah, the girls were so cool. This film I remember we were producing and we had great music and everything, but we didn't have a hero. We sent it to Imran Khan who was taking a lot of time reading it, and then said, 'Listen, it's nice, but it's not that great,' and I think Dinesh (Vijan) had offered it to Ranbir Kapoor without telling me. I was the producer.

Yeah, this is what happens when you don't pay attention to your business, but I think he forgot Ranbir is my cousin-in-law, who told me later. He said, 'Yeah, it was nice, but...' Nobody wanted to do it.

AC: Really?
SAK: Yeah. Imran didn't want to do it; Ranbir didn't want to do it. So I said, 'Okay, I'll do it. Let's just make it.' And it worked out well. But this wouldn't have happened if I hadn't said, 'Let's

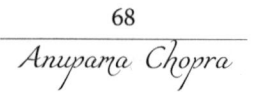

shoot it,' because they weren't able to find a male lead.

AC: But Saif, for about ten years now you have played this multiplex hero. Were you, by this time, a little jaded?

SAK: Yeah, maybe, sometimes there were scenes and a writer like Imtiaz (Ali) would bring something new to it. I think if you keep changing as a person, that automatically brings something new to the same scene, but if you're not careful, it could have a repetitive kind of vibe to it. I think I had sensed that I need to try and do something new, which was actually why I was trying to put Agent Vinod together, which didn't work out, but I mean it's a well-produced film and if it had worked... It was a kind of an attempt for a guy who does romantic comedies in doing something a little more age-appropriate.

AC: Right.

SAK: In your early 40s, you can be a RAW agent or whatever. I don't know how many of these attempts at manipulating one's fate actually work, but that's what it was. But I thought this would be pretty much the last time I'd be doing it also. I kind of sensed it.

AC: Did you know that?

SAK: Yeah, I felt it. I think I was getting a little bored also, of...

AC: When you were doing it?

SAK: Yeah, of that vibe. Imtiaz, as I said, had some fresh lines, but generally...

AC: I remember. *Aam aadmi* (common man), remember that? Mango people?

SAK: That was *Love Aaj Kal*. Which was also nice, but the soul of the romantic hero is a guy who's confused about his future and is commitment phobic. And I think that's really irritating after a while to the audience. The guy has grown up, been married twice, and is still confused? He shouldn't be.

AC: Right.

SAK: Yeah, it's a young man's world.

AC: Right.

SAK: It suits young kids to be like that. I don't know, but young men should know.

AC: Correct.

SAK: Yes, that's that as well.

AC: Which brings me to *Go Goa Gone*, which I feel was the beginning of the new Saif, the sort of Saif 2.0, where you start to kind of really experiment.

SAK: Yeah. I don't know how much we experiment or when people come up with something new. I think there has to be a synergy and a confluence of ideas where the audience has to be ready for something new. Then someone has to offer you something new and then you have to take it. You get offered stuff, so timing is critical in stardom and movies and success, and you have to be in that zeitgeist or whatever, you have to get it right. I really can't, I feel, be the engineer. You have to be the right guy at the right time in any kind of stardom situation. Whether it is cricket, sport, and film, I think it's about being the right person in the right place.

AC: But Saif, by the time this came along, you were ready to be this blonde, wannabe Russian, whatever he was.

SAK: I actually dyed my hair for real but it went kind of carrot. Because from dark brown to blonde, carrot is easy to end up at, but I was committed to it. Yeah, there's something in my mind where I just said okay. It's a profession and it's a scary profession and it's fraught with superstition and ideas, but the idea in any creative field is to not be scared, and if you can manage that, then you have a bit of an edge. So, if you're not worried about failure and if you're not worried about money and if you are really concerned about creating something new and interesting for the audience to watch, that's the place to be, where you're willing to go out there and say, okay, let me dress how you want or to let me try and really do something new without being afraid. I think that's the key.

AC: Which brings me, Saif, to your current triumph. Let's go to the next one (a bearded and turbaned Saif pointing a gun in a scene from *Sacred Games*).

SAK: I remember this shot. I asked him for one more. This is a moment where I shoot this guy who's running away, and there's this whole thing happening about shooting unarmed suspects. But he's killed my friend, so it's easy when I have a gun in my hand, and to try and go into a certain mode of being this cop or detective, and bring real emotion to it as an actor because that's what you have to convey all the time. The story is, I shouldn't shoot this guy. He's unarmed. And then I just can't help it, and this rage surges through me and I shoot him anyway and then go there and finish him off. So, to have a story on your face and in your mind while doing action was growth for me as an actor. They were okay with one take and I asked Vikram Motwane, 'Can I do it again, please, because this is what I'd like to add to it?' And he said yes, of course, and we did and it seems to be an image that's endured. So, great!

AC: What I loved about Sartaj, Saif, was how human he is and how flawed and frail and sad and even overweight. There's one episode in which I think it was Parulkar who says, '*Haan, weight bhi gain kiya hai.* (Yes, you have put on weight as well.)'

So, Saif, are you completely removed now from the trappings of stardom? Is there no vanity about this anymore?

SAK: I really want to be in a place where I can say to a director, 'What do you want from this guy?' I love having a creative job, okay. I love that feeling of staying up late at night, like last night, looking at a script and saying okay, let's make something out of this. And then going to sleep and waking up to Taimur, and my wife and everything's nice. I don't want to feel stressed by the job and, as you say, affected by the vanity of it.

I want to just become what that character is, for a while, really enjoy that, get paid, and take off. So, I don't know whether the entire definition of stardom has changed. I don't think I'm being that different; I think that's the way it should be for stars. They should become that character, if it's fat or if it's thin, and people have blazed the way. I mean Aamir, as usual, has shown that that's the way to do it. People don't really tell us very often what the path is, but it's clear for people who can see it. And one of these things is—the actor should become the character, and that's quite starry as well. It's a luxury...if you're not doing twenty things, and if you can afford to say. I mean, putting on weight is easy, just eat pizza, but to maintain it or to become really thin for a part, I mean, that's great. Now I think it's the future and the present of cinema where somebody says, 'You're playing a Naga Sadhu and I want you to be a little underweight.' And you say, okay, let's...What kind of diet would my character have? Oh, he'd eat an onion and a roti. So will you do that for your part? That defines you.

AC: Saif, you had said in an interview that, 'I think more like an actor than a star.' Is there a big difference between the two?
SAK: Well, there shouldn't be, but...

AC: In our country there is.
SAK: Of course, there is. Because a star implies that there's money involved. In the sense that whether there are other brands you're sponsoring or stuff like that or the amount of money that a film is going to sell for because your name is on it. So there are financial considerations. This is what I think is the main part of being a star, not just having an attitude at a party. This is the age where the actor is kind of responsibility-free. Like a good actor can come onto a project and play the main villain in your film and it doesn't really make so much difference to the box office, whether he's there or not, unless he becomes a star. So the difference

between a star and an actor is the financial difference it makes. Having you on that project is, what I feel, apart from the aura around you. I mean some people have that glow and shine, but that's monetized usually.

AC: So, at this point, do you think of yourself as an actor more than a star?

SAK: I don't think I have a choice.

Yeah, it keeps changing with me. There've been times when I've been in a fairly commanding position as a star, and there've been times when I haven't. But I've always tried to improve as an actor and I'd like to think of myself as an actor. When we first joined the movies this wasn't even an industry, like it wasn't recognized by the government. I think that happened very recently, so in our passport forms, when we had to fill in the profession, we'd write 'actor', but we were wondering if anyone took that seriously. But now I think of myself as an actor.

When I'm not working, I read books on acting, I try and improve my craft, and I think about it much more than I ever did before. The kind of work we're being offered is also really different and exciting. So, yeah. I don't want to be a star in that sense because I find it very tiring. I've seen a lot of stars. I still see stars around me.

AC: You're married to a star.

SAK: Yeah, married to a superstar and my mother was a superstar and my father was a superstar. But he was very cool, compared to the actors, because they're very worried about hair and makeup, and my mum used to be in a very bad mood when she'd get ready. We couldn't go anywhere near her, so I instinctively loved and hated that as well. I think it's important to be normal and be an artist and enjoy the art of it, rather than the vanity of it. The dark side is annoying to me. 'I'm better-looking than you and hope you die,' kind of thing. I mean, nobody admits to that.

AC: But it is there, isn't it?
SAK: I think so, I think it is. I went through getting over it when I realized I really can't benefit from anyone's failure.

AC: But there are moments when you wish failure on people?
SAK: Not wish failure on people but if something goes wrong you're like… Aww.

AC: Right, right because it is that kind of business. I mean it is…
SAK: You have to know some psychology to understand this. They say that when some people fail, it implies there's more room for others to succeed. So that's the thought, whether you understand it or not, you'd feel that you've just been given an opening, whereas the more successful other people are, the more it closes off avenues to other people; so nobody really loves it. That's the thought.

AC: When did you realize that you can't benefit from it?
SAK: I don't know. I was in my 40s in the late 90s or something when Sanjay Dutt was arrested. I don't know, something happened, something big happened. It didn't change my life at all, and I said, 'Oh, the only thing that can help me is me. This really won't help me if these top three guys are kidnapped and taken to Mars…' Maybe that would help actually. Maybe it would…but short of that… Anyway, and it's not a nice feeling to be negative about. It isn't. It does eat away at you slightly. It's better to be focused on yourself and try and say, 'Let me be the best I can be.' Yeah.

AC: When you talk about the 90s, Saif, you often say that there was no connect between you and the films.
SAK: I had no idea what I was doing. Yeah, it was amazing. Like I would say these lines, but I honestly had no idea what I was doing.

AC: What was the funniest line you had to say?
SAK: I remember so many of the lines from those days. I had to say something, something like, '*Ki saboot ke taur pe, bande ki chaal, chaalu nahi damdaar hai* (For evidence, the stride of the

man is strong, not cunning),' and I was like what does that even mean? But music used to be amazing in these movies.

AC: Absolutely.

SAK: I would work very hard—before people start thinking I had everything really easy. Saroj Khan used to tell me, 'Turn off the lights on the set, tie a malmal on your head, and get it right—you're not changing a step—and we'll go and have lunch.' And I'd be there in the corner, trying to do this for hours, and I think audio saved me because I had a weak voice, and particularly because it is difficult to be a good actor if you don't understand what you were saying, but the songs were good in all these movies, so I became a dancing hero in the 90s.

AC: So, Saif, but even now when I see your interviews and you're talking about wanting to play Dorian Gray, and I just think, how does this guy fit into Bollywood? How do you?

SAK: Well, I think Bollywood, that term, it's good now, but, I think, it's a pretty demeaning term. But like the Impressionists and the Protestants and a lot of these terms originally were meant as an insult and they just...

AC: They just stuck.

SAK: They stuck and are being worn quite proudly. So it's a big umbrella, Bollywood. There are so many different kinds of people. It's not just Dharma and Yashraj. I mean there are different production houses doing such different kind of stuff. I mean, *Masaan* is a Bollywood movie.

AC: The definitions have changed.

SAK: Yeah, so there's room for all of us if you can just be yourself. I think that's the great thing about the profession—we all speak the same language when it comes to cinema. So, you can be as alien as you want in your personal life or in your taste. You can't help where you've grown up. Most of us have something in common. I don't feel I'm that much of an outsider, but certainly in some things. I don't really feel that it's an issue anymore. I think I have plenty of people that I can talk to.

AC: You feel at home?
SAK: I do. I feel very much at home, I mean, but if you put me in a genuinely academic situation, I don't feel at home. If you put me with Oxford graduates who are law students, I'd feel—okay, these guys are a bit too bright for me. So, I have often thought this is where I do feel at home, on a film set with these guys, just the right amount of art and the right amount of having fun and being a bit silly. I mean, these are my kind of people also.

AC: I remember a conversation we'd had after, I can't remember which wedding it was, but there was some wedding at which you performed.
SAK: Oh!

AC: And then you said, 'I'm never doing that again.'
SAK: Oh!

AC: Was that just very difficult?
SAK: Well, I don't know. I was doing one wedding and my aunt came backstage. She was a guest, and she said, 'What are you doing?'

I said, 'I'm dancing on stage.' She said, 'Oh God! Please don't. They're all my friends.' So, yeah. Back in the day, some of the Pataudi aunts used to have an issue with it; the Bengalis were fine somehow. Look, some of these weddings are like shows.

AC: Right.
SAK: They put up these big mandaps. It's not like you're doing cabaret in their living room, but sometimes it is.

I think cabarets in the living room should be avoided, but that depends on who you are and on how much money you have, on how much money you want, and on how you value yourself, and what you think of yourself as. Some people say, 'I'm an actor, I can't see myself doing that,' and I think that's a cool way to think, and there are other guys who say, 'Look, we're entertainers, and that's what we do.'

AC: Yeah, Shah Rukh says that. He's very clear about it.

SAK: Yeah, it's fine, and I think that's great and Shah Rukh's got, well, I shouldn't say what I was going to say.

How do I say without saying it? Like Shah Rukh has done very well for himself. He's got a big house, let's say that. I won't say where it is.

AC: Right.

SAK: But he's converted his time into great success and he's still doing it, and I think that's amazing. So, to each their own. That's the point, but also I've never basically been comfortable dancing. It's weird for a guy to be an amazing dancer.

AC: Why? After all those bleeding knees and all…come on!

SAK: Yeah, but those were different steps. It's just, I think cool guys shouldn't be able to dance too well; they can dance a bit, but they shouldn't be like, 'Wow, look at me.'

AC: Have you told Hrithik Roshan that?

SAK: Yeah, but they are elastics. I don't know, that's my take on really good dancers. I'm more like the Ajay Devgn school of dancing.

AC: Very controlled.

SAK: Very controlled, yeah, like how guys should be.

AC: Too macho to dance?

SAK: I think even the girls are nervous dancing with Hrithik. They're like, 'Oh my God! He's so beautiful.'

AC: He is.

SAK: Everyone's just looking at him.

AC: So, Saif, do you miss being a producer, controlling the material, creating material?

SAK: When I'm not shooting, I do miss producing, because you come down to the office and you make these decisions and they're quite creative, like what font should we write 'Go Goa Gone' in? Should it be silver or should it be red? And what should the poster look like and how should we do this, and which film are we making? I didn't really like how much we are paying the light guy and can we get cheaper plates for lunch? That's not my kind of conversation, but the guy who has that conversation ends up running the production, though, so I do hope I can do it again. It's a very creative job. It's a producer-driven industry actually.

AC: And you're enabling storytelling.

SAK: And a film should be a producer's dream and idea, and then he puts everyone together and says, this is how it should be, so I do miss that, yeah. I look forward to doing it again.

AC: You will?

SAK: With all these, with Netflix and things like this, there's a high chance that... I mean we've already spoken to them, saying, let's try and come up with something that we could produce. And they're open, so I'm having a good time acting, but I do miss it slightly. I live on the tenth floor of my building, the second floor is the office, so it was great. I'd come downstairs in my pyjamas and sit there and have these chats about the future and that used to be really fun, and I miss it.

AC: But you think you will get to it?

SAK: Yeah I'd like to do it. I don't think I'm very bad at it either. I think I gave our company a good direction with films like *Go Goa Gone* and *Love Aaj Kal* and I thought even *Agent Vinod* was a good idea for a movie that went wrong. I'm sure it's the right kind of movie, in a sense.

AC: You said, Saif, in an interview, that it's a blessing to like your wife; not everyone has that luxury.

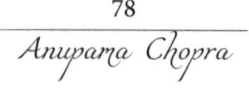

SAK: I should really watch what I say more often. It's a blessing to be loved.

AC: But to like your wife?

SAK: Yeah, I mean we all get into relationships, but I think after a while things change, and so do people. I mean, when you're in love, you don't even realize that you're two different people, and then when you start realizing you're two different people, it doesn't suit everyone all the time. So, to actually like a person is something else, where you like certain things about them. You say, 'That's great, and I respect the way you live your life. I like you like a friend, as in, I would like to be around you because I can't be you.' That's the thought, right? So yeah, I think it's lucky, obviously it's lucky. I can well imagine a lot of people not liking the people they're stuck with after a point because you can't afford to keep getting divorced.

AC: That's right. That is true. You also said that if interesting offers dry up, you'll go and garden in Pataudi.

SAK: I keep saying that and I hope I can do that.

AC: But could you walk away like that?

SAK: I mean, if there are no offers, I can make an art form out of living life without working. I'm still from the P.G. Wodehouse, Bertie Wooster generation. You need money, but mornings should be about reading the paper in bed, breakfast, a little gymming, lunch, some time with kids, family, gardening, maybe jujitsu, something...I don't know. Actually, I remember my father saying this line whenever he would get fed up. Cricket was also very political, more towards the end of his career. He was a very big star and the cricketing world revolved around his aura in Bombay in the 1960s. But in the early 1970s, when it was ending, there was politics and this and that and he'd say sometimes, 'I'll just leave it and go to Bhopal or go to Pataudi.' And I have this image of the nawab sitting in his palace and saying, 'I'm not bothered,

I'm gonna do something else.' He left these four letters to the selectors. He said, 'I quit,' and my mother called them and said, 'Don't deliver the letters; I'll sort him out.'

AC: Really?

SAK: Yeah, and she followed him. I think he started drinking a little early in the evening and said I'm done, and she said, 'No, no, I think my life will be affected, so you have to...' So she kind of got him back into the game for those five more years. But I'm just saying that's stuck with me, his ability to say, 'If it all gets too much, I'll just go to Pataudi.' And it's like a haven; it's peaceful, it's quiet and it's lovely, so it's a thing, I'd say. I probably don't mean it, but one day it will happen and I think one day I will. My grandmother used to grow these roses and used to really impress me with...I don't know...grafting buds, where you take a bud from one plant then make an incision on the...

AC: Cross-pollination type?

SAK: Yeah, and then stick them on, and I'd be watching her. So, these are just ideas for retirement, because she was old when she was doing that. So, it would be nice if I could do that and not get too attached. Like I said before, things run in terms of decades. You shouldn't want to be thirty when you're forty-seven. You should move on to other fun things like living your life in a slightly different way. I can easily do that. Yeah, but I do love working and I think the material is becoming more and more interesting. So I don't see why not now, with trailblazers like Mr Bachchan...Rishi Kapoor also just did a good movie. If you're a good actor and if you know your stuff, I think you can keep working. I'd like to keep working.

AC: So, guys, we're going to let Saif go. Thank you so much for coming for the interview.

Thrilled to speak to Ranveer—an endlessly fascinating artist, impeccable dresser and a great talker.

What fun in my first 'Adda' session with Anushka Sharma, Varun Dhawan, Sriram Raghavan and Navdeep Singh!

Varun speaks about his work in Badlapur; *director, Sriram Raghavan, looks on.*

To mark Anushka completing seven years in Bollywood, we discuss everything from drinking to producing, to Virat Kohli.

I was afraid that people might not be interested in a controversy-free conversation with Kangana. However, we have a great time chatting about what acting means to her.

I ask Priyanka what she has had to sacrifice along the way, and she says, 'her life.'

I try to strike a regal pose with Sanjay Leela Bhansali on this stunning chair from the film Padmaavat.

As always, Shah Rukh speaks candidly, and goes from wit to depth in a nanosecond.

Saif Ali Khan is articulate, witty and always great to interview. When an aspiring actor in the audience asks him for help, Saif replies, 'Let me help myself first!'

'When in love, even water tastes like sherbet,' says Ranbir Kapoor.

Chock-full of anecdotes, Hrithik Roshan tells me how he tried to find a safe career before plunging into acting.

In conversation with the very witty Abhishek Bachchan on Manmarziyaan, *his hiatus and everything else.*

Beneath The Surface

Shah Rukh Khan

Almost twenty-seven years and a hundred credits to his name, Shah Rukh Khan has had a glorious career. He is charming, a little cocky, very funny, relatable, and somehow, still larger-than-life. He believes the only cure for failure at work is more work, and the only cure for success at work is more work! That also explains how SRK has kept going from the time he made his acting debut on television in 1988.

Shah Rukh spoke to *Film Companion* for an extensive four-part interaction on love, life, family, kids, stardom, friends, peers…and even crossdressing! He even let the world know about his biggest nightmare—making small talk over text messages or emails!

Years ago, Shah Rukh told me, 'I am just an employee of the Shah Rukh Khan myth.' I've been having conversations with him since 1995, and he remains one of my favourite interviewees.

PART I

AC: Shah Rukh, you know, this is the twenty-first year of our conversations.

SRK: Oh wow! We have a whole book to prove it.

AC: I first came to you in April 1995, on the sets of *Ram Jaane*.
SRK: That long back?

AC: That long back. You were wearing a purple suit.
SRK: Yeah, I still have it.

AC: You still have it?
SRK: Yeah. You know my Kolkata Knight Riders? That's why it is purple. I'm inspired by my purple suit.

AC: By *Ram Jaane*?
SRK: I met a bad guy who had seen *Ram Jaane* and he got so disturbed the way I played the bad guy. He asked me, 'Which bad guy have you seen who doesn't wear a shirt under a suit?'

AC: That's right.
SRK: *'Aisa dikhta hoon main* (Do I look like this)?' He got so angry. I said I'm really sorry, I'm new to Mumbai. I don't know the bad guys from Mumbai.

AC: Your portrayal was not on point?
SRK: Yeah, he got very disturbed that I was wearing a gold chain and said, *'Hum aise flashy hote hain? Woh shirt kyun nahi pehna tumne* (Are we this flashy? Why didn't you wear a shirt?)' I was, like, okay.

AC: So you said things like, 'I've four or five expressions, people think I'm gimmicky. Balls to them,' which I thought was very funny. This was, of course, pre-DDLJ's release, but my sense is that inherently you're still that guy. You're still charming, a little cocky, very funny, relatable, and somehow, still larger-than-life. Is that a correct assessment? Are you still that man?
SRK: Uh, I am. I mean, people don't really change. People talk about evolving in X, Y, Z, but there are certain beliefs that we live by. When we are younger, maybe, it seems even stupid, so you talk

more like that. Well, I think what you say in your childhood or youth is who you are. You may garb it in better speech patterns. I mean, I don't say 'balls to them' anymore. I just say, f*** off.

AC: *(laughs)* You're just a more polite man now.

SRK: I am just polite now. So please, will you f*** off? So I don't use language like that anymore, but I think, somewhere, whether that belief was misplaced, whether that belief was right, whether it was something that comes instinctively from inside, I think that's who you are, because sometimes you'll see...

AC: That's your essence.

SRK: Yeah, that's your essence. Like you meet your son and you'll be chatting. And how old is he? Eighteen now?

AC: He's going to be.

SRK: And he'll just say something and you're like, how can you talk like this?

AC: Yeah! All the time.

SRK: It's not right. But he will be that person. Of course, he'll curb his way of talking. Of course, he'll understand better, but I think the essence comes out in that period of life which kind of defines us finally. But deep down inside, if I take off my shirt, same guy.

AC: It's appropriate that we're having this conversation in Lisbon while you're creating a love story with Imtiaz Ali and Anushka Sharma. I mean, you've spent half your life playing a man in love.

SRK: With women who belong to other men, to begin with. I was just telling Imtiaz and Anushka, just before the shot. I just told them I've made an art and profession out of loving women who are going to get married to someone or already married or are engaged, and then I run after them. And then I get them from wherever they are, from any corner, sometimes with charm, sometimes with goodness. Sometimes I throw them off the building. But yeah.

AC: But you get them.
SRK: I think I have a problem.

AC: Let's accept it.
SRK: You have to accept it. I have to accept it. It's a problem, it's chronic and I need to do something about it, and the only thing I think I can do about it is just keep doing it again and again. Maybe one day it will get rid of me.

AC: But Shah Rukh, has your understanding of love and the portrayal of it in Hindi cinema altered a lot? Or do you find yourself going through the same beats?
SRK: It'll sound a little pompous and all-knowing, but I know all facets of it. However strange it may sound when I say it. While doing interviews, I'm very honest, so I'm telling you. It's a shocking thing, like you might find a person who knows all the theorems, you may find a person who knows all the plays of Shakespeare, and you'll find a lot of people who have all the knowledge about films. I am a lot like that for love, I honestly am.

AC: What does that mean?
SRK: I'm beautiful, not physically only, I mean in a different way. I'm unpredictable, I'm charming, I make you glow, I make you sad, I destroy you, I distress you, I create longing for you, I create belonging in you. I can be the worst thing that happens to you; I could be the best thing that could happen to you. So I'm genuinely like that, and I believe in love like that. And not just a man-woman love or man-man love or woman-woman love, of sensuality. I think even...

AC: All kinds of love?
SRK: All kinds of love. I know love very well, so I understand Aditya Chopra's love when he tells me to do *Dilwale Dulhaniya Le Jayenge*. I understand Imtiaz's love. He told me once, 'Sir, I was a little wary about what I'll tell you about love, but I suddenly knew what he means and where he is coming from without wanting to

know his back story. All of us have a back story, which we kind of expose in our cinema, especially the writers and directors. Actors still less. I'm not saying I'll be able to deliver just because I know love, because obviously I'm bound by my five expressions, but I really, really need to say, 'Can I sense this? Can I feel it? Can I hold myself back?' Adi would do the scene like this, Karan (Johar) would do it like this, Imtiaz is going to do it like this... so I get really intrigued by it. It's fortunate and unfortunate that if you try something completely in a dark space in a love story, I think people will get a little...

AC: It'll be too shocking.
SRK: Yeah, they'll be like, '*Arre nahi* (Oh no), you shouldn't do it like that.'

AC: I mean, when you did *Kabhi Alvida Naa Kehna*, when you went into that hotel room, people couldn't believe it was you with somebody else's wife.
SRK: Yeah. And just to let you know, it was a body double, it wasn't me.
I don't do love scenes or kissing scenes either. And I see movies, everybody is doing it.

AC: That's right.
SRK: Yeah. I was really taken aback when people reacted to that film, and I think, as an actor, it was a very nice, cynical, angry character. I remember somebody saying, '*Woh toh uske face pe dikhne lag gaya hai* (It has started showing on his face).' So I kept my face in angst all the time.

AC: I saw Suhana in a school play and she was really good! And so I tweeted about how she was really good and you tweeted back to say, 'It's the same face, but I have so much to learn from her, she has so much more brevity and grace.' Do you think that, after all these years, you still haven't quite cultivated enough brevity and grace?

SRK: No.

AC: Really?

SRK: Two things have happened, Anupama. When I see someone like Suhana, I mean, obviously, there's a bias or whatever people may think because she's my daughter, but some young actors, like Alia—I've just finished a film with her—and I get so amazed by the lack of life they have lived, but they can still express so much without knowing all the expressions of life or having felt them. My assumption is, I think, that Alia hasn't, Suhana hasn't (seen life), there's still more to see. You always say, when you see life then you experience different things. I mean, without having the experience and still being able to convey emotions. I would take much longer because it is perhaps that my experience has given me more expressions and my brevity is gone? You see, craft is tangible. It can bind you. There's a method to it. Art is free-flowing, that's how we believe art is...

AC: Instinctive.

SRK: Instinctive.

But craft, as you go by, starts binding you, so it stops being that free-flowing, because you start thinking of so many things to fix it, make it right, get the point through, make it stick. Like Anushka and I were just asking, 'Is it right?' We start asking that too often as an actor, but when I see Suhana do what she does because she's still not bound by the craft, and hopefully before she gets bound, the art would have taken wings. I think I've been given that opportunity. I'm not cribbing.

I think I have that opportunity, but naturally, I think, the craft coming in binds you and then the nicest way to deal with it is to work with people who are not bound by the craft as yet, have free-flowing art and then imbibe what they're doing. I think Alia is very good. I think she's really new. Amongst the new people, I haven't really seen too many people or worked with them, actually.

AC: But it genuinely makes you happy.

SRK: It makes me happy obviously. I don't like many actors. I have malice towards one and all.

AC: (*laughs*) Why?

SRK: All actors have that. It is just that we're very nice and all. Somebody told me, politicians all around the world abuse in public and hug in private. Actors all around the world hug in public, and abuse in private. So actors have malice, and it's good malice. It's not bad malice. They're not like, deciding to stab each other. I think I have the ease now. I don't have to prove it. I don't have to get it right, so I'm like, okay, let me just come in a scene. I'm not ill-prepared. I think I just need to know my lines. I need to know my points of focus. I need to understand what the scene is going to convey.

AC: I was reading something David Fincher said a couple of years ago, 'I'm not interested in movies that entertain.' He said, 'I love movies that scar.' He said, 'What I love about *Jaws* is that I could never swim in the ocean again.' Your, of course, sort of forte has always been entertainment, but after all these years, do you want your cinema to do something else? Do you want it to scar, to educate?

SRK: If one can place it like how David Fincher has...but I think *Jaws* was extremely entertaining.

AC: No, no, of course it was.

SRK: Yeah, you can find a deeper meaning in your cinema as time goes by, and you can only find it post people have, sort of, decided what they liked or disliked about it. See, I can't make up my mind...

AC: You can't do it before?

SRK: You can't do it before. I don't think so, but I wanted *Fan* to shake you up and entertain you as well. God, if this happens! It's just a scary thought and it is an interestingly scary thought, and it can actually happen to me, not that it has, but it can shake you up a bit. Suppose a guy looking like me gets completely taken in and obsessed, and I meet people who love me so much. I keep telling people, those who look like me or want to look like me, 'I love you all'. It's really not only just complimentary, it's just so honest and earnest. When I was young, I thought I looked like XYZ.

AC: Your mom thought you looked like Dilip Kumar.
SRK: I thought I looked like Mr Bachchan. Later on, girls said I was like Al Pacino, so I got the best of them all.

AC: No, but don't you decide primarily, I want to entertain, that is my sort of reason for being?
SRK: I think, for twenty-five years, and genuinely I say so and I don't just have this stupid belief in myself, I've never thought of a film as an entertainment medium. I'm like, 'Let me just do it. This is fun.' Like I think this film that Karan has made, *Dear Zindagi*, maybe I'll be lynched for it. '*Shah Rukh ne ye role kyun kiya* (Why did Shah Rukh do this role)?' People have a lot of things to say, but I think it's very interesting.

I think it's a very nice film to be made, and if I can add to it by just learning this new experience, because perhaps I don't have the age to do a full film like that anymore, or stage, or my stardom is too big perhaps, or whatever the reason is. I just haven't got an offer like that. It's interesting to be a part of that film and let's see what it does to the world. I mean, I'd be lying if I say that I'd like my cinema to be like that, and not commercially successful. I would like that too.

PART II

AC: So these people who are sort of forming images about you on social media, or talking to you, saying, 'Why did you do this,' how much attention do you pay to all of this?
SRK: I can't pay any attention. Not because I think it is meaningless,

or I think that it's not worth a listen. But I think a lot of stuff on social media is just...I mean you just hear and you just have to let go of it. Sometimes, a very small thing is made out to be too big... But I guess now it's handled, I have enough fans, I'll just write to them, 'Come on, tell them it's not true.'

AC: So you sort of mobilize the armies?

SRK: Umm...I mobilize love.

AC: Shah Rukh, when you're at a stage when you make a decision to do a film, it sort of changes the ecosystem of that film. Right! So it's so important what you commit to and what you don't commit to. So, how much do you actually think through before you say yes or no, or is it purely gut, even now?

SRK: Purely gut.

AC: Even now?

SRK: Yeah. And that's what I like. I say yes to a film and then my well-wishers and friends will just turn over and say, 'You don't have to do this, yaar. Why are you doing this? *Arre tu yeh wali kar na* (Oh you should do this)!' Like I'm doing Aanand L. Rai's film now and everybody knows I'm a dwarf in it. But I'm told, 'Why would you be a dwarf?' We like to see you like this only.' And it's going to be very difficult. I mean, six-eight months of hard work, and with my knees, and VFX, and I've just gotten out of *Fan* which took the mickey out of me. It was really difficult to do. I just do it by gut, yaar. I don't have any calculation. There are days when a film doesn't fare as well as I think it should have, then I'll be like *'Yaar, main calculate kar ke kar raha hoon* (Oh, I will think through such things in future), but I can't do it, yaar. I couldn't do it in the beginning, I can't do it now. When I started off, I think I was the right guy at the right place, at the right time, maybe. Things just fell into place. There were good directors. I don't take credit for all of it. I'm just hoping it will continue like that and if you can be lucky once, you can keep on being lucky.

Why be negative? If you got it right once...

AC: Twenty-five years!
So, I saw the graduation speech of yours at the Dhirubhai Ambani International School, and you talked about... I'm going to completely mess up the pronunciation, the German word. *Kya tha woh* (What was it)?
SRK: *Zugzwang.*

AC: *Zugzwang.* And you said it means being in a situation which you really think you'll never get out of, and you're like, 'Damn! I have to get out', and you said, 'Ask me, I've just made *Dilwale* and then followed it up with *Fan*', and you said to the kids, 'Make a move, and with a little bit of embarrassment, it'll pass.' And I thought it was an amazingly sorted way of handling things that didn't go the way you wanted them to. Did it take a while to get to that place?
SRK: One, let me be very honest, because I had said this to the kids, so I won't lie to them ever. There is no other alternative if you fail. If you're in a spot which is between the devil and the deep sea and it goes wrong, there will be a little bit of embarrassment. Embarrassment is an extremely self-inflicted issue. The truth is really that not very many people are actually bothering about what's happening to you, not very many people. So it is self-inflicted, but still, it exists. Just because it is self-inflicted, it does not mean you don't feel embarrassed.

It's a chess move, *zugzwang*, and if you suffer a little bit of embarrassment, just do the thing that comes to you. If it goes wrong, just move on. I really believe that the only cure for failure at work is more work. The only cure for a success at work is more work. So there is nothing else that you can do but bloody work. And that's the only cure I find. Let it be something of a reminder of how you felt for those days. Let it teach you, let it make you remember that, 'Oh, I don't like that feeling.' And if you hit failure hard enough, then you won't fail again.

AC: I have seen you talk about things I've said fifteen years ago. You still remember lines people have written about you. Don't you think somewhere that's just holding onto stuff that you don't need to? I mean, isn't that negative?

SRK: No, no, no, no.

AC: No?

SRK: No, I think I'm an extremely positive person. As a matter of fact, I think I'm so positive and polite that people may take it as a weakness. A lot of people do, because I keep quiet, and I overlook things, even in the various departments of my work, which I should be looking at, maybe more carefully. My strength is the fact that I am frail, and I know it. All of us are. Yes, I don't stand in judgement, for sure.

Yes, like any human being, I'll get angry with people, I get disturbed, or have a thought that, uh, this is not right. And yes, when you wrote what you wrote, I held it against you, because I thought that was unfair. But fair and unfair, after some time, from whose point of view? You're a journalist, you're a writer, you did your job thinking that was the best line you could come up with. I thought to myself, I felt closer to her than this—she could have given me that much leeway. Whatever. But I don't hold it against you anymore.

Like that whole scene we finished just now. Cameraman Mohanan came, the director came, and Anushka came, and quickly they got it over with, because I know they also don't have to share this with anyone else. And if you're an actor, and I've been doing it for twenty-five years, sometimes it seemed like really, really stupid and mundane to be saying, 'You know, Aryan, I got that!'

'Yeah, Papa, that's your job.'

'I mean, really, why are you getting so excited about it? You do it well.'

So I don't know how to share that moment of happiness and I don't how know how to really sit down and explain; this is what I feel about a film, in spite of and despite what people write about it, or think about it, or thought about it, or analysed about it. This is what I felt when I went wrong as an actor because nobody understands that. Maybe a co-actor does...

AC: So do you share?
SRK: I think, for so many years I have kept things to myself, that I have stopped sharing. I'm still caring, but I've stopped sharing.

AC: That's just a default mode now?
SRK: Yeah, because I just feel it'll pass, it will just move on and I need to keep it within myself. And it's not just the failure, sometimes the sad parts, the good parts, not being able to explain to people, where you are seeing the world from. It's not such a f*****g special place.

AC: It is!
SRK: It's not really, yeah. It's not.

AC: Shah Rukh, there are women here standing and waiting. There's a whole line of people up there.
SRK: And how many women can you have?

AC: (*laughs*) God! Like what a big problem. Right?
SRK: No, and the thing is that, perhaps they don't even know me. I mean, I really (*laughs*) sometimes want to sit everyone down and say, 'Listen, if you got to know me, maybe you won't like me at all. You don't know me!'

A lot of people say to me, 'I'd like my son to be like you.' A lot of actresses have told me that, 'I want to grow up and be like you,' and I say, 'Please don't wish for that, because you don't know me, how it is to be me, unless you spend time with me; be with me and realize it. Really, I mean, he is okay. The highest point in his life is catching Pikachu and Pokémon. And we think he must be having the most exciting life, like, people think, 'Wow, he must be having a gala time in Amsterdam, partying away.'

And I am sitting in a car in a cold place, and I'm trying to catch Pikachu. And that's the highest point in my life. I'm not cribbing. It's great to be a movie star and it's great to be in my position. And you even get used to people loving you for so long, so if somebody doesn't love you, it's like, 'What? Why don't you love me? How? How is that...? Me?' Everyone likes me...

AC: I'm the best thing since sliced bread (*laughs*).
SRK: Yeah, everybody is not supposed to love you, fool. That's what you keep claiming...you're a normal guy. Then why are you behaving abnormally? But not in this case! You've got to love me, everybody loves me, so it's a difficult place to be in, yaar. I'm completely living in a bubble, and I love my bubble. I am okay being in it, and I just can't explain my bubble to everyone.

AC: So maybe, maybe you and Aamir and Salman should sit down, because you are the only three who have experienced this.
SRK: Actually we have never spoken about superstardom.

AC: About how famous you guys are?
SRK: No, no. Sometimes we speak about how we can make a difference working together, but those are only the good things—we speak a lot of dirty shit also.

AC: (*laughs*) I can imagine.
SRK: I am joking. I didn't say this about Aamir, okay! Aamir is a good boy. But the other day I was sitting with Salman, my son and I had gone to see him late at night. And he said, '*Kya lucky hain hum log yaar* (How lucky we are)!' God has given us so much. At our age people are readying themselves for retirement. We are really fortunate. Come on, let's have a drink. But I realized, when he is saying something like that, it has a strange amount of familiarity, that is, how grateful we are.

I know, a lot of people—my friends, my family, they turn around and say, Shah Rukh, you've got to be grateful, God has been so kind to you. I can't explain to them the gratitude I feel.

But I understand when Salman says it. But I'll be very honest. In the line of work we are, if you're not late sleepers like me and Salman sometimes, you hardly get time to meet each other. And if you do meet too often then people say that maybe you're having a relationship, and this is one last rumour I want, that Salman and I are in a relationship. That's the only thing left now. But yeah, it's fun when we sit down. I do take the time out to go see him and he takes the time out.

Aamir, when he is working, he is extremely proper, *ki nau baje so jaaonga, main nahi aaonga* (I'll sleep at nine, I won't come) and all, so we don't meet him too often. But yeah, I spent an evening with him and Tim Cook and that was nice. I think I have said it in your book before. Sonny Liston, he's the one Muhammed Ali beat the first time, wasn't very articulate. He would say, 'Ho, yo, hmm', and suddenly Muhammad Ali came on the scene where he was, like, 'Fly like a butterfly, sting like a bee...I'm so beautiful, I'm the greatest.' I mean he was like talking, walking, handsome... And here was the other boxer, who's a world champion, but he just spoke so little, he just grunted once in a while.

And then one day, they spoke to him, and they asked him, 'Did you feel that he used to speak so much and that made people like him more?' And he said, 'Sometimes, so much has happened in life that you don't find words enough to articulate that. I come from that life.' I still do the same forward flip over the sofa for my third child now. I play the same game. I go and buy the same toy. I am doing the same stuff. I'm still doing the forward flips, even now, after 25 years, and maybe, I'd like to believe, with different nuances.

PART III

AC: So, before we broke off for you to do the shot, you were telling me about the superstar experience and how you can't really tell anyone what it's like.

SRK: Because even I don't know.

AC: No, it's your life.

SRK: You can't... It's not very explainable to be honest.

AC: Sure.

SRK: I can be modest and say it's a regular life, it's very normal, but obviously it's not normal.

AC: Is it always enjoyable, though? Or does it ever get exhausting?

SRK: No, there is no other place I would rather be. Yeah, I'm very clear about this. I mean, I don't think about it, I don't get depressed, I don't get nightmares thinking what if I wasn't a star anymore? I never have. Because of what we decided twenty-one years ago, I believe.

This is going on. If it goes on for twenty-five years, then what is there to check or crosscheck? I love being loved, I love being a big star, I love being in the public eye. I love being criticized, I love being controversial. I love being Shah Rukh Khan.

AC: A couple of years ago, I was listening to Javed Saab at the Jaipur Literature Festival and he was talking about lyrics, and he said this, '*Maaf karna, lekin tehzeeb thodi kam ho gai hai hamare gaano mein* (Pardon me, but our songs have lost their decency).' And I felt like, it's not just the *gaana*, it's everything. In life, *tehzeeb thodi kam ho gai hai* (We have lost our decency in general). I mean, you just look at the sort of public discourse, the slanging matches on social media. When two films release, it just gets ugly. I mean, why this lack of *tehzeeb* (decency)?

SRK: I'll tell you, we haven't lost respect for each other, we've just lost self-respect. It is very strange. There were things I would not hear or say. When you're talking about public slanging and the way people talk... How can a self-respecting person speak like this?

AC: Yeah.

SRK: It's not whether I respect you or not. That's secondary. If I don't respect myself, how do I get up in the morning after having spoken like this about someone at night? I think we're just losing self-respect and dignity. I mean, just because we say, 'You go girl!', 'Say what!' or 'Yo! Wohoo!' it doesn't mean anything. We're expressing ourselves in exclamations now. And exclamations are actually shocking alphabets or whatever they're called.

AC: But you think it's because bad behaviour gets attention and everybody wants to be in sort of...?
SRK: I think people mistake bad behaviour for honesty. I'm saying it like it is. No. It's not like this. Give it a thought, man. Maybe it's not like this. I read somewhere, one of the gentlemen, one of our colleagues working with us somewhere started writing some really strange things about my colleagues—Bhatt Saab and Karan. He used to work with us. We love him; he is a singer. He writes some strange stuff and says, *'Main sach bolta hoon* (I tell the truth).' No, no. Saying it like it is is being rude. You're mistaken, and it's sad because then I find people retaliating.

AC: Yeah, yeah. It just goes on.
SRK: Then some regular guy, a normal person, also starts it. And I'll tell them, come on! Let it be. Actually, just being honest to God, whenever I've done it, I've apologized. Whenever I've had an outburst, I'm really apologetic. I'm really apologetic to myself and to the world for setting a bad example. And this is not a justification, and this is no excuse, but all of that builds up sometimes, as a public figure, and it comes out in that one little incident. And then, yeah, you're retarded, and you're supposed to be mad, and you're supposed to be pompous, and you think you're a big star. This is no excuse, no excuse. I should not even do it then. You need to, I guess, take some Prozac, some calming medicine or something. I think I should be taking rest a lot of the time.

AC: Meditate, practise mindfulness.

SRK: I should, really. I think very often that I should learn cooking, gardening, so I'm trying to learn how to make Italian food. Tonight was for pasta. Honestly.

AC: What rubbish! Really?

SRK: I swear, I swear. I want to learn how to make Italian food. I want to cook Italian.

AC: Why?

SRK: Let me clarify on your programme, it's not because of my political affiliation. I want to cook Italian—I think it's very sexy.

AC: It is. Listen, any man who cooks is sexy.

SRK: And I've got all the other sexy qualities.

AC: Correct!

SRK: I've got a tattoo also. So I want to wear an apron, and pour some wine in a glass, drink from it and cook food. I know it's very sexy, but I want to do it for my kids. There's a lady here, Letti. She's teaching me. I learnt it before for about five days but I've forgotten now. When my shoulder was broken, I took time off and did it, but I really want to do that and learn ten songs on a guitar and sing to every woman in the world. Whoever she is, whatever age she is, whatever stage of life she is in. I want to know ten songs to sing and a guitar, an open jeep, Italian food, cooking abilities.

AC: That's it.

SRK: Looks, I have! I just...

AC: Full seduction, right?

SRK: No, no, I'm a complete package. Come on! I deserve to be a superstar. And, and I'm humble.

AC: You don't want to be applauded for that?

SRK: At my stage, no. At my stage, I don't want to surprise you. I don't want to shock you. I don't want to be shocked by myself.

In Conversation with the Stars

I'm not in a hyper place anymore. But it's not about proving something to anyone anymore. It doesn't take away the edge, doesn't take away the competitive spirit, doesn't take away the yearning to do something really new and fantastic, which I've never done before, and it's not about being able to prove it to my three-year-old son when he turns fifteen...that is why your father is so famous. Because he deserves to be, not because of a film called *Dilwale Dulhania Le Jayenge*, which he did twenty years ago, and it still runs in the theatre. That won't work for him, maybe fifteen years later, or maybe it will, the way it is going.

AC: Listen, I just went back to see it. It still works, man.

SRK: My sixteen-year-old daughter says, *Kuch Kuch Hota Hai* has such sweet songs.

AC: Yeah.

SRK: So, my logic is, if I want to innovate, and if I want to do something new, I'll have to do it for that three-year-old, four-year-old, and I'm really, really full of energy for that. When I started off, I told everyone, I want to do five great films. And when I say great, greatness is time-bound. Things change. Five years later what you thought was great is not great any more. But still I want to do five great films. I think I've not even done one.

AC: Really?

SRK: Yeah, they're dated now, they're finished, they're done. And once greatness is done, it's no longer great actually. Greatness is when you haven't done it and you're pining for it, yearning for it, wanting it. And at this stage, I'm really, really hungry for greatness, in a good way. It's really, really sad if I feel, 'Do I deserve this?' even for a moment. I should genuinely believe that I deserve a few things—I don't want to have too many. Though I talked about politeness and courtesy, I don't want to say thank you to anyone, I don't want to owe it to anyone, and I don't want to say sorry to anyone.

AC: It's true. It's your own hard work.

SRK: It's my hard work. I've worked for it. I went wrong and I tried it. I know it sounds like too much of 'I', but I'm being honest in saying it, and I don't want to say sorry to them that I've let them down, that I screwed up. These are two words I don't want to say at the end of my career. Sometimes, in the last six to seven years, I think my physicality has stopped me because of injuries, but I've overcome them. You saw me slide?

AC: I did. Pretty good!

PART IV

AC: Earlier we were talking about *Fan*, and about your superstar life and I wanted to just show you one of my favourite scenes from the film.
[A scene from the movie *Fan* plays.]
I love that expression on his face when he is screaming. You talk often about not knowing what's real and what's unreal any longer. And then you do a film like this in which there are versions of you—there is a fan of you and there's you, of course, acting these roles. Did it give you any insight into your own experience or into the people who stand outside, all those women we saw just waiting today?

SRK: One, it proved to me something I have always been scared of—schizophrenia. So, after this film, I know that I'm 100 per cent schizophrenic. 100 per cent, there is no two ways about it.

AC: You had told me that great story about Javed Saab saying, 'How are they?'

SRK: He always calls me SRK-1, or is it SRK-2? I chanced upon this little word that somebody mentioned to me once, where I'm so emotional and I'm so detached. So I'm demotional.

AC: Is that a real thing?

SRK: I think it's a real thing. I'm demotional. I'm emotional about things, I'm over-sensitive, and then I'm very detached from all this, so for me the mindset is demotional. Specifically when I was doing *Fan*, there were moments while doing the scenes where I started crying, and not for the scene. And I was not meant to cry in some scenes but I had a lot of issues... when the superstar was to play the fan, playing him.

AC: Right.
SRK: That was really awkward, and I'm very proud of that scene. When I come in, and act like him acting like me.

AC: Yeah.
SRK: How he does the stage show mimicking me.

AC: Yeah, that is just another level of hall of mirrors, na?
SRK: Yeah, it was just completely... And I would cry doing it. I have never been so frail as an actor. I have succumbed to the emotion. I have never been the actor who cries on the sets and then says, 'Yeah, give me a moment.' I don't need a moment. I do this. I'm a professional actor.

AC: But why can't you be frail?
SRK: I am doing my job. I'm frail in private.

AC: But don't actors have to be frail?
SRK: You can't be frail while doing this interview. You have to ask what you have to. Suppose you suddenly start weeping and break down here, because it's not going the way you wanted...

AC: (*laughs*) That would be really funny.
SRK: So we can't do that. I'm an actor. I'm supposed to come and cry. You have to be very honest about being an actor. A lot of the bravado, lot of the stuff that I do on stage with the immense amount of confidence I have is, I think, 90 per cent what I'm not. It's a desire to be that person. I've got a lot of complexes, obviously inferiority being top of the list. I have so many issues

with my physicality, and that's why I'm so bloody confident on stage. And then post the release, when it didn't do well, I cried a lot (*laughs*).

AC: Did it really break your heart?
SRK: Yeah, yeah. When films don't do well, it breaks my heart. And I know some of them are not good enough, but this was extremely special. And there were a lot of analyses on why it was wrong, and maybe they are right. But analysing an emotional moment is kind of awkward and strange for an actor. So yeah, it broke my heart.

AC: But does it make you afraid of trying something new again?
SRK: Every time I fail, I'm such an impudent, incorrigible and uncontrollable, arrogant, self-centred human being. If you tell me not to do it, I will do it again. And I will do it worse, if need be. And when *Ra.One* didn't do what I thought it should, I'm going to make it. And I'll be in a wheelchair, but I will be a superhero. I'm not letting go of that. I will get it right. I cannot let it go wrong. I just read a saying while in the car, 'If you throw me to the wolves, I'll come back leading the pack.' And I really believe that, and I'm not being pompous and giving a star statement. I'm not happy that I failed. I wish I had done it right, and that wouldn't have stopped me from doing newer things, but this encourages me even more. Heartbreak is followed by, 'No, I'm not letting go of this.' Because *ab to toot gaya* (Now it is broken)...

AC: *Ab kya hona hai* (What will happen now)?
SRK: *Ab kya ukhad loge* (What will they do now)? And I don't hold anyone responsible for it. The audience has the right to kick you in the butt, and critics too. You don't like it, you don't like it. I can't force you to like something of mine. I like it and because of my liking it, it just broke my heart. And now that it is broken, now there is no stopping, because nothing worse can happen. Now I'm dangerous. So every time I fail at doing this,

if you want to control me, then let me just succeed more and more. The simple mantra.

AC: The Lincoln Centre gave this tribute to Tom Hanks, and Julia Roberts said, 'Tom Hanks can walk into any room and make people feel comfortable.' She said it's a true gift and I think that you do that too. How do you do it and how have you maintained this quality through all these years?

SRK: To be really honest, there is a word in Urdu called, '*Mehman-nawazi* (warm hospitality)' and if you come to my place, I just need you to feel important because I like thinking that everyone likes feeling important. Not in the way that you are the greatest ... and... I have been accepted so well by so many people with such varied tastes and I think so less of myself, and if you could make me feel nice, how little does it take for me to make everyone else feel so? I genuinely go out of my way to do it. As a matter of fact, when I'm really down and out, I meet people. When I say people, I don't mean friends and people I know. I just want to go out on the streets and meet people. I want to touch the people whose lives I think I may have touched, because they genuinely love me.

AC: So you work at it?
SRK: Now it has become...
AC: It's just who you are.
SRK: Also, my father was like that. My father was always very, very kind, courteous, loving, sweet, told stories, made everyone laugh. And I know that I walk with the tag of a status now, and I don't like it. I don't want the status of my stardom to be my tag. I want the status, 'He's a good guy, man. He's a normal guy.' I don't wear my stardom like a tuxedo. I wear it like a T-shirt. And that's how it should be. If you are a real star, you don't need to prove it in any other way than just being kind, gentlemanly, normal and cool. And I may not be, and I'm not socially very good, so I lose all those people who I meet at night because I haven't messaged

them or returned emails the next morning. Some really, really good people, and they hate me for it, but I can't help it. I don't know how to do this, saying, 'Hi, what's up?' or 'Thinking of you, saw your picture on the poster, looking really cool, and last night was great fun.' It was great fun, you know it.

AC: But you are done.

SRK: No, no we are done. I don't have to now write it down and email it and make you feel really good about it. I hope you really had a good time last night. I had a great time. Hope you got some sleep. You must have slept.

Just because you had a good time doesn't mean that you won't sleep. You sleep, everyone sleeps, and it's your space, and it's your time, it's your place. And then I send an email and that person is like, 'Oh ho, I have to send one back.' They say, 'Yeah, great fun, got to do this again sometime.' I say, sure. And then how do you end it? My biggest problem is how do you end an ongoing communication on a tablet, or a telephone or an email? I have no idea.

AC: Smiley emoji.

SRK: Which I can't do, it's too un-macho for me.

AC: Hey!

SRK: I mean, death before smiley.

AC: Oh no!

SRK: I told you I'm not rude, so I don't know how to do this. I'm like…in the middle of the conversation, so, yeah, cool, yeah. And I write big messages if I write a message. So I'm not into okay as 'K'. So I really ask people, how do I end this?

AC: When we were doing the book, one of the things you'd said to me was, 'I have always put Shah Rukh before the superstar Shah Rukh, which is why the superstar keeps prospering.' You said, 'I have my heart in the right place, which is what you need as an

actor.' Have you managed to keep your heart in the right place?
SRK: I think so. I think so. I mean, I read so much about me, and I may be doing something.

AC: Do you read about yourself?
SRK: Sometimes; it is unavoidable.

AC: But you don't actively sort of scout information about yourself?
SRK: No, no, no. I'm not so self-obsessed yet. There might come a time when I start getting them marked, but I can tell my team to mark them in yellow markers wherever my name comes, wherever it is coming. It can happen.

AC: There was some award function where you were dressed in drag, doing a pole dance. Why do you need to do that?
SRK: I don't know. It's, maybe, a desire to cross-dress and do a pole dance.

AC: I was just watching that. It was you and Ranbir, and I was like, what are these guys doing? Why are they doing this?
SRK: You got me here. I want to cross-dress and do pole dancing. It's my thing. I do it at home. Whenever I see a pole or a saree...

AC: You just leap on it?
SRK: I leap on it. I'm a closeted pole dancer. You got me there. This is it. Nobody knew the secret. In my bedroom I have a pole running through my bed, and I wear my wife's clothes.
    Yeah that was bad, that was in extremely bad taste. That's the worst part about being on celluloid. It always comes back to haunt you.

AC: It does. It is all on YouTube. You're not getting away from it.
SRK: And I didn't even have six packs then, so even my midriff was so bad. Yeah, it was not nice. When you are doing things, sometimes you just say, let's do this, man. Let's kill it. Why not?

And just this creative, emotional instinct laced with a few drinks.

AC: And before you know it...you are a woman.

SRK: And because I believe in equality, I think you should not look down upon me just because I want to be a woman. Because I question you all, all right! You can't do this. My children appreciate it. It was the high point in their life. Sometimes they introduce me to their friends like this. You see that in cross-dressing pole dancer? That's my dad. He is a world famous movie star. And he does that at home.

SRK: I think that was in bad taste. I think Ranbir is okay doing it. Me? Not. I think Ranbir is alright. I'm going to call him and tell him. It was okay, it suited him. Hold it against Ranbir if you have to...

AC: That's right. It's all his fault.

SRK: All his fault. Really, he could have told me. He's been in this, his whole family has been in the business. Come on! I'm a newbie. I came from the outside. I don't know the ways of the industry, and they exploited me.

AC: Your sense of humour has gotten you into trouble, okay?

SRK: Now I have learnt. See, I don't crack jokes. Smileys are going to sue me after the show.

AC: Do you hold back?
SRK: Yeah.

AC: Purposefully?
SRK: Unfortunately, it's very boring. I stopped doing some of the hosting. People have become a little touchy about things. They get angry. And earlier... I don't know what it is. I thought with time people will develop a better sense of humour from a person who has done it regularly. And I'm very self-deprecating. Extremely. 80 per cent is about me making fun of myself, and then maybe a few jokes, but yeah, I hold myself back now. I have been

warned by my children. I have been warned by my friends. They say, 'You are not a stand-up comedian. Shut up'. So yeah, I hold myself back. That's why lately I'm not as funny as I used to be.

AC: You are pretty funny.
SRK: I know, but I could be funnier. The world has lost out. Imagine... And cross-dressing, it will never be repeated again.

AC: In an interview that you did with Ankur Pathak for *Huffington Post*, you said that as long as you are making movies, there are going to be people waiting outside Mannat to see you. Is that something you truly believe or is it sort of, *dil ko khush rakhne ke liye khayal accha hai* (It is good to have such fanciful ideas to make the heart happy)?
SRK: It's a belief. When I started this interview, I told you, when you are young, you have some very stupid things to say, some stupid beliefs, but they are beliefs, they are the essence that you live with. These are the things which define you when you grow up and you speak a lot and you speak a little stupidly. And like you said, you don't speak like that anymore, and you have changed, and stuff like that. And I say we are better suited now. It's a belief I have had, that if I joined cinema, I wanted to be the biggest star in the world. I may become that, I may not become that. I may never be as big as I thought I would be. Like your son right now believes that he will be a better cricketer than Virat Kohli, and he will. There is a difference between belief and faith. I have faith actually. Belief can be questioned, has to be proved, it can be done in a theorem in Mathematics. Faith is like faith in God. Faith is unshakeable. I don't know whether I will live long enough to see this, but it will happen. I don't know what you guys might be doing; you'll retire and go away, not get a job, but me...

AC: I'm here forever.
SRK: I'm here forever, cross-dressed or not. I'm here. I'm not going anywhere.

On Dominating the World

Priyanka Chopra

*P*riyanka Chopra did more than break that proverbial glass ceiling in Hollywood. She starred in a TV show with an ensemble cast, was on the cover of a host of magazines and even made it to *Time*'s 100 most influential people list.

Already a formidable star in India, Priyanka Chopra migrated from the Mumbai film industry and has made a name for herself in Hollywood. Today, with two movies and a new YouTube show, Priyanka persists with her world domination plans.

●

AC: Priyanka, first I will tell you that your success makes me ridiculously happy. I was thinking this morning, why do you make me so happy? Because you were a big star even before *Quantico*, it's not like you need validation from the West necessarily. Of course, this is another level of world domination. Let's accept that. But I think what's really amazing is how you've totally subverted the Hindi film rule that women in their thirties are past their prime. Your success has actually, in a sense, shifted the goalposts for success.

PC: I was just being an actor, doing my job. I thought of it as just an extension of myself creatively. I did not think the show would explode the way it did, I didn't think that I would get the kind of response I have in America and around the world because of the show, and somehow, a response to me, not just my character.

AC: Yeah, yeah, it's to you.

PC: Yeah, to me as a person and as an artist. I'm just so grateful that it's broken so many different barriers and stereotypes on so many levels because that was my aim from the time I did *Aitraaz*. I have always tried to push the envelope a little bit, especially when I started in the movies in the early 2000s. The girls were always…pretty, which is amazing as well. I love doing it and I love my saree blowing in the wind and I love the boys serenading me. I love all of that, but it was just limited to that.

When I was told, at a very young age, at about nineteen or twenty, that, *'Ladkiyan to interchangeable hoti hain filmon mein, agar dusri heroine nahi mili toh nayi ladki launch kar lenge, kya farak padta hai* (Women are interchangeable in our films; if we don't get a heroine, we will launch a new girl. What difference does it make)?' I think subconsciously it really stuck in my head, and looking back retrospectively I made my career what it is because I had something telling me that I will not be replaceable, I don't want to be replaceable. So, it is surprising that not just as a woman but as an Indian actor, now that I've worked abroad…I've realized that Indian films are really not looked at with as much respect as they should.

AC: Really?
PC: Yeah!

AC: I mean, what, it's just kitschy?
PC: They're like spoofs of Hollywood and breaking into song and dance.

AC: Yeah, Anurag Kashyap had told me it's seen as the variety entertainment of global cinema.

PC: Yes, it is, and I didn't realize that. When Mr Bachchan, Shabana Ma'am, everybody was talking about how they hate the term 'Bollywood', I didn't get why. After working there, I hated it too. I've denounced it.

AC: Really?

PC: I'm not saying it anymore because we are not a copy of Hollywood. We're an extremely prolific film industry, and I know, Indian actors get foreign films all the time, we get approached for them. I did, at least, for the last four or five years, but everything was the exotic princess or the beautiful girl standing behind a guy, and I've always wanted to be more than that.

Not saying that there's anything wrong with standing behind a guy, but to at least have quality within that... So, when I spoke to ABC as well, and they came to me with this deal, they said that they believe that I was probably one of the few Indian actors they've seen who would not be too alien for America. Yet, we are interesting enough to be able to not crossover but to be able to appeal to a mass audience, and the only thing I told them was that I'm not going to do 'Oh, here is my big fat Punjabi wedding', or here is 'Let's dance Bollywood'.

AC: Like the obvious stuff.

PC: Why should we just be that? I said I want to be cast on merit, one, and second, my ethnicity should be just because it is.

AC: Right. It's not a thing.

PC: It's not the reason why I am where I am, and kudos to them, they found me. Every script that they gave me, all twenty-six of them, none had anything to do with my ethnicity. Alex was not even written for an Indian girl, and on top of that I told them, I'm really sorry, but I'm used to playing leads. Even if I play a supporting part, it has to be something that is going to be one of the most integral parts of the show.

Otherwise, I have an amazing career. I'm not looking at doing anything different, and they understood that. Recently, as a joke, when somebody asked me, 'Oh, there are rumours about you becoming the next Bond girl.' I said, 'Please forget Bond girl, I want to be Bond.'

AC: I saw that. (*laughs*)
PC: It was an interview at 11 o'clock at night and I was being my...
AC: Like this one?
PC: Yeah, this one. I was being my sassy self. Sass comes out at night for me.

AC: But tell me, how do you become such a huge success on social media? I mean, even your armpits get talked about.
PC: Listen, my armpits were on CNN in America. It was so funny, People magazine, TMZ... *In India toh chalo khair I am Priyanka Chopra from India, so chalo they'll write, kyunki I belong to them* (In India, it's okay because I am Priyanka Chopra from India. They will write because I belong to them). But I was amazed that the news was carrying me, and this was while I was in Paris. My publicist Dana and I were sitting and saying, 'Oh my God, they're carrying this picture everywhere', and everyone was freaking out and the whole team was saying, 'It's becoming such a big deal'.

I was thinking, *kitna photoshop kiya unhone* (How much did they photoshop)? So I showed them my real armpits. I said, see it. Chhee, I hate the word also. I am feeling shy saying it. I was like, see it, so she was like 'true', so I said, 'You know what, let's end this. Let's just do a picture, show what they really look like, and then compare it.'

AC: Actors are now being asked, don't you want to do what Priyanka has done? So, it's become a theme now. Do you look back and say, wow what just went down here? Do you pinch yourself?
PC: No, I actually have worked very hard.

AC: Yeah, this hasn't come easy, no?

PC: It hasn't. You can't just go to America, sign a movie and become a Hollywood star, and I'm not saying I am. I'm not even talking about my film *Baywatch* right now because it's not released. That's not even in the debate about my achievements. My achievements are because I work sixteen-hour days for five days a week, and on the weekends, I used to come back to India and shoot *Jai Gangaajal* and *Bajirao Mastani* and go back for Monday morning shoot. That's the only way I have worked even in India, so I don't know what to do if I have two days off.

I just love what I do and I'm good at it and I love the ability to wake up in the morning and say, 'Oh my God! I get to go to work.' I mean, how many people in their lifetimes do a job that they love doing? Most people do it for survival. *Ki acchha* (yes, okay) we need to feed our families, we need to survive, it's our career, okay we have to do it, but to wake up with my feet and fingers tingling, and say, 'Wow, I have this to do, I have that to do today,' it's an amazing feeling, and I don't take it for granted.

Yes, it's a lot that's happened very fast. I mean, whether it was the *Time* cover, whether it was the Oscars, or the Correspondents' dinner, or at least the seven covers that I've been on recently only in the US, not even talking about India. All that is just about 1 or 2 per cent of what talent, good talent deserves in global entertainment.

AC: But Priyanka, tell me, you brought up *Time* magazine...
PC: I jumped with happiness.

AC: Did you not?
PC: I did. I'll be honest. I was like...what? I remember, when my publicist emailed me, saying, you're being considered, because their voting and stuff was going on for the 100 most influential people. I was thinking, 'Wow, I'm being considered.' That, in itself, was the achievement for me, that I am in consideration with this lot of people. Then to be a part of the list, then to be on the cover

of the magazine, not just in Asia but in the US as well. And then to have my Padma Shri within ten days.

AC: That's right, Padma Shri Priyanka Chopra.
PC: Yeah, that one week was a real big 'pinch me' moment.

AC: But tell me, there's of course, the sweat. I mean you talked about your days flying here for a weekend. But what is the sacrifice you made to achieve this?
PC: You sacrifice your life!

AC: Really?
PC: Yeah, your life is your work, completely. I get to meet my friends in Bombay only for the twenty days that I might come here now, for this year at least. My family, yes, I can fly them down. To be in a completely new country, get to know new people, reintroduce myself and see if these are friends for life or not... It's not just the fact that that's all I do, but it's such a solitary thing to do.

My grandmother passed away this year, not because she was ill or anything, but because she was ninety-four or ninety-five. I was so afraid while I was shooting Season 1 (of *Quantico*) that something would happen while I would be away, and I was very close to my grandmom. She raised me till I was about eight or nine. I was so scared that I wouldn't be able to come for her funeral, and I arrived, we celebrated her ninety-fourth birthday, and four days later, she passed. It was almost as if she was waiting for me. So I can only talk about my journey. It is very solitary; sometimes the noise, the sound of silence is too quiet.

AC: So, even now, Priyanka, there's no sense of entitlement?
PC: No, I don't feel it.

AC: *Thoda sa star sa you don't feel* (Don't you feel even a little like a star)?
PC: No, I have a sense of pride definitely, because somehow,

with re-acknowledgment of the fact that I have consistently done good work, because of which I have a sense of self and a sense of pride. I'm unapologetic about who I am, where I've come from, or what I've done. I can stand on any global stage, talk to heads of states, or talk to film actors or prolific directors, or I can make conversation because I know my job. I may not have been able to do that six years ago because it took me a while to find my own, but yeah, I don't take it for granted. I was very fascinated with show business. When I joined the movies I found so many sad stories of people who, after they've become superstars or they realize that they're superstars, have a downfall. It's going to happen to everyone. Everyone.

I knew that before I started my first film, so I'm not afraid of it. I just know that I'll have a Plan B when that happens. Creativity can be morphed into so many things. Today I write; I sing; I write columns, I have written for *Elle*, *The New York Times* and *Hindustan Times*; I act in movies; I'm producing films. There are a gazillion things you can do as a creative person, so I'm prepared for that. But I do believe you can't ever sit down on your hands and say, 'All right, now I am a star.' That doesn't happen to anyone, and people don't forgive that, because they have put you there.

AC: And you never let yourself have a slightly arrogant moment?
PC: No, arrogant I can get sometimes.

AC: What do you do?
PC: I think I'm self-assured; people call it arrogance, so I don't know. Sometimes, when I have my 'Masaki quips' (*laughs*). But that happens to me usually at press conferences where people are trying to instigate me, so then they'll say, oh she is arrogant, but it's not so. I'm self-assured to a certain point.

AC: So I've read this column where I can't remember the exact words but they were talking about the fact that you were on the

cover of *Time* and they said it's amazing how far a great publicist can take a mediocre actor and how deeply even mainstream journalism can fall for it. Do you ever respond to stuff like that? I don't mean literally, but does something in you kind of react to it?
PC: No, yeah it made me feel great. If my mediocrity could come to *Time* magazine, then I mean, no wonder it hasn't happened to anyone else before me.
Arrogance or self-assuredness? You pick (*laughs*).

AC: We think of the West as more educated, more evolved, more egalitarian, but I interviewed Melissa McCarthy and Paul Feig for *Ghostbusters* last week.
PC: I'm so psyched about that...

AC: Me too, me too. I'm dying to see it.
PC: I cannot wait. They better get it right. Otherwise no female will ever be able to do a male protagonist film again. It's just so cool that *Ghostbusters* is being made with women.

AC: Exactly! But Priyanka, Paul was talking about the levels of trolling, misogyny, the kind of hate that's come their way.
PC: 100 per cent.

AC: So, is it not that different?
PC: No, it is not; entertainment is not different at all. First of all, I do not know why we always come from a place of second. We absolutely shouldn't. America has never been the end-all of entertainment. It's just one of the biggest industries because they speak in English, and yes, they make amazing films. Their way of storytelling is different; our way of storytelling is different. There's no comparison.

AC: No, but in terms of gender parity, they are not so much ahead of us? I mean, I was so shocked hearing this.
PC: Look at the kind of debates happening with the presidential campaigns right now. We had a prime minister who was a woman

way before. When I made the James Bond comment, so much of trolling I got, that there can never be a woman James Bond and that he is James Bond, how can you kill the sanctity of that? I actually think it'll be quite cool.

AC: It would be.

PC: Whether or not I do it, some girl should do it. And her name should be James, it shouldn't be Jane. I think the world has come to that place because the fight for feminism has a lot of voices now, yet, we live in a world of misogyny. It is not India only but it's a global issue. It happens all over the world, because for eons, women have been told they're second class citizens. And now suddenly, what are we asking for?

Feminism has got such a bad name now, the term, because people think feminism is berating men or hating men, which it's not. Women are only saying, give us the ability to make our own decisions without being judged. We want the freedom that men have had all these years. That's it, but it will be a big war.

Feminism needs two things. One, for women to encourage each other. Instead of pulling each other down we need to prop each other up. Girl love is very important. And second, feminism needs men to stand up and say that this is the right decision, and hopefully we are walking towards that. It's not going to happen instantly, it won't even happen in the next ten years, but the debate has become strong, the conversations have become strong.

We are seeing *Ghostbusters* with three women in it today. When I did *Fashion*, people laughed at me, people told me *koi nahi dekhne jayega aapki* film (nobody will watch your film). *Hindi actresses tab karti hain* (Indian actresses do these movies) *when they're at the end of their careers kyunki unko na National Award vagairah chahiye hota hai* (because they want a National award). That was like 2006? And now look...

AC: It's a different world.
PC: That's what I'm saying. So, it's brave steps by brave women,

female actresses, who have come out and said, 'We are going to take this chance; we will be the only face on the poster and you will watch it because it's good content.'

AC: Well, more success to you, Priyanka, and to the armpits.

PC: It's so invasive...it's private (*laughs*).

AC: (*laughs*) Thank you so much.

PC: Thank you.

Undiluted and Unstoppable

Kangana Ranaut

Kangana Ranaut has been in the news for various controversies, but in this conversation, we focused on what acting means to her. She discusses actors and directors, good, bad and indifferent, as well as her penchant for speaking her mind and not caring about who she offends.

In a room full of film aspirants, Kangana talks about what she's done to better her craft, how she has managed to bounce back from failures, and a backup plan if her movie career fails. Her films reveal her as an artist with boundless ambition, and I am excited to see what she creates next.

AC: Kangana, welcome. I am so thrilled to have this opportunity to talk to you in a room filled with aspiring actors. I am hoping that the conversation we have here about your incredible journey and your incredible talent will inspire them all to work harder.
KR: Thank you, Anupama! Thank you so much for inviting me. It is a pleasure to share my techniques with you all, and I hope I will be of some help.

AC: Kangana, since we last spoke, you have been mired in controversies. There is a writer who says you have stolen his film, there is a director who says you have stolen his...umm... film, again, then there is nepotism which keeps going on, and then there is, of course, the whole Hrithik Roshan thing, but I don't want to talk about any of that.

KR: Thank you. (*Kangana bows to Anupama, and everyone laughs.*)

AC: What I want to know is how, as an actor, you can disconnect from all the sound and fury and just focus on honing your craft.

KR: I think, guys, you all are from a film or drama school, which I haven't been to. I have met some incredible actors over the years, and from them I have learnt the exercises they did in school. Piyush Mishra told me how important yoga was for actors. It sounds a bit lame to say meditation is very important to stay focused and to have clarity of mind.

Maybe there's a controversy and people know about it, but something or the other will always be imbalanced (in life). So, I rely a lot on meditation and so do some of my friends who are theatre actors and come from drama school. I myself have done theatre, and my exercises are mostly yoga, but 'dhyaan' (meditation) is a very important part of it. I mean it's called 'dhyaan' for a reason. So you have to concentrate, and it is projected onto what you want it to be projected on. It is very easy. Especially for actors.

What is acting? Acting is meant to build your impulses and your emotions to arouse yourself to a situation, unnaturally. It is not natural. If you want to cry, you have to be in an environment that will make you cry like a normal human being, but as an actor, you have to create an imaginary environment to cry, to arouse yourself and stimulate your senses to be able to get to that level of emotion.

Over a period of time, what happens is that unnatural stimulation causes a lot of emotional, very abrupt...what do you call it...meltdowns! If you are happy, you will go sad, if you are sad you suddenly feel happy. If you are an 'aware' person then you will know that it is because of acting.

If you are in a van right now, you have to jump out of the van, and then do a laughing scene...what will you do? You will make yourself happy, you will start to jump and think of all the things that make you happy or you do this for sadness. Your mother is dying, or something. So, there is so much (happening) and you stimulate your mind so much that you start to feel a bit emotionally unhealthy.

I think actors get a lot more emotional than most people, and the more they act, the more emotional they become as people. That is why a lot of them are twisted...(*smiles*) in reality and sometimes enter very doomed kind of circumstances and have an unhealthy emotional life. So, what can happen with controversies and even in your personal life is that things might affect you either not at all or in an exceptionally extraordinary way.

AC: I know you are not on social media, but do you, when you are in the middle of a role, let's say, while creating a role like Simran, disconnect from reading about yourself?

KR: Ideally I should be disconnected all through the filming process, but sometimes you cannot afford that. But what is very important for me and very crucial are the initial few days when I am tapping into the character. Sometimes when you are getting into the character and trying to discover her, it needs a lot of concentration, and you cannot afford to have your concentration diverted anywhere else. The quickest I have done it is with Datto (the name of the character from *Tanu Weds Manu Returns*); I think it took me around ten days to get into that character. Then it was like, 'Oh! I have her now', and the longest time has been with *Manikarnika: The Queen of Jhansi*. So, yeah, as long as it takes! So, if it took me, say, two days, then yes, post that I can be myself. I can search myself on Google and see what's going on.

AC: Making notes?

KR: (*laughing*) Yes, and sometimes it is also like…I have to finish this script quickly so that I can go back to all these websites—the fashion websites and all that stuff.

AC: Do fun stuff…

KR: Yes, do fun stuff. Do frivolous stuff. Yes, that is a difficult part.

AC: Kangana, I was talking to Nawazuddin about how he creates his characters, and he told me how he actually takes things from his own life. So, the scene in *Gangs of Wasseypur II* where he is asking Huma Qureshi's permission to have sex with her was actually an instance from his own life.

Now that you are co-creating your characters in a very proactive way, is there a part of you in Simran, or Rani or Datto?

KR: As an actress, as a performer, yes, there is a part of my personality in these girls. And in terms of thought, there is something that I feel strongly about. With Simran, I felt it was the story of a girl who wanted to be rich, but I, on purpose, pushed her anger into a role…this particular role…this woman's. Simran became a person who enjoys having sex, because I felt it is important for our nation to come to terms with the fact that a woman also wants to have sex.

AC: Oh no! Who knew!

KR: So, I felt, with my own personal experiences of our society, it necessary to put it out there that it's perfectly healthy and normal for a woman to want to have sex, especially for those who are sexually active. So, she doesn't find shame, and this is something I forced (into the script). She doesn't find shame in picking up boys; she is single, she has dated many men, and she is just divorced. She has dated many men, and she takes pride in that. There is nothing wrong in that, and so, I think it comes from my concern for my surroundings, and this has been quite a concern.

Even with all the talk about women empowerment and feminism, we are not able to give our women respect and a certain comfort with their sexuality. For example, when I was hurt in *Manikarnika: The Queen of Jhansi* by a sword during a sequence, a lot of people from my crew came up to me when I was bleeding. Apparently, I was very brave in the way I dealt with it, so they came up to me and started saying... 'Oh, you got balls, you got balls,' and I said, 'No, I don't have balls.'

AC: (*laughing*) The last time I checked...

KR: (*laughing*) I have a vagina. Why can't you say that word? Why is 'balls' easier to say than vagina or ovaries? It's so cool to say 'I have ovaries!' So I think it has been taken away from us. Our sexuality has been taken away from us. Same goes for 'pussy' or 'sissy'. It is associated with cowardice. Women are associated with cowardice. I think that is horrible.

You can carry a human being in your vagina, so how can it be a sign of weakness? So, there is a lot of brainwashing, and I want us to be free of that. We should go beyond all this now. To consistently talk about equality for me, in my thirties, is becoming embarrassing. I mean, of course we are equal!

AC: Yes, that's a given.

KR: It is embarrassing to be fighting for equal pay and equal work, or even having sex. It is not about vagina or balls, it is about me as a woman wanting to join the army, and my lover wanting to be a poet. Come on! It's not about vagina or balls; I think we should go beyond these prejudices and yes, coming back to the point, I take the liberty of just injecting these little things (into the script).

AC: Coming back to Simran, you said in an interview, that when Hansal (Mehta) came to you with that project, you said that you didn't want to have a director-actor relationship; you wanted to be a partner. But, Kangana, even the most talented, most successful actors in Hindi cinema, you know, Aamir Khan, and Shah Rukh Khan, talk about submitting to the vision of the director, while you say you are fed up of taking directions. So, how does your relationship with the director work?

KR: I am fed up of taking directions from egomaniacs because it doesn't come with…I mean…I would love to be under the supervision of somebody who gives me a sense of being equal. Just taking instructions from someone doesn't mean that they can be dictators. I feel, with direction, there is a lot of confusion. Most people tend to be dictators. Like, I remember this director who would come every morning and say… 'Then I want you to… in this line look down…this line look up…this line you exit…'

You can't tell me how to act, because I am an actor. You can tell me to do something else, like ask me to interpret it differently. The best directors that I have worked with say, '*Thoda ek notch higher kar do* (Take it a notch higher)' or '*Thoda kam* (Tone it down)'. This is the best direction you can give to an actor. You can't tell an actor to mimic you. Another director I worked with told me, 'Look, anything that you want to do with your character, tell me in the van. Don't talk to me in front of the crew. The crew respects me.'

So if I want to tell my director something about my character, like I want this line extra or maybe I am sitting here on a chair and saying this…we should see how it works. So, I can't have this conversation with my director. Apparently, it is hurting his male ego. But honestly, I prefer this one to those who have hostile impulses and release them on actors at the wrong time and wrong place. This is much clearer and nicer. It is (like saying), 'Hey, it really hurts to know that you also have a mind of your own, but can you sit in your van and I will come to your van everyday…?'

AC: (*laughing*) *Dimaag sirf van mein dikhana.* (Show your intelligence only in the van.) Are you serious?
KR: Yes.

AC: Really?
KR: I can go on and on… So what do you do? How do you work

in an environment like this when you have had enough of it? There was this time when I said to myself, 'Fine. There will be a day when I will be free of all this. So, I have to give myself the comfort of that freedom, that is, if I can afford it...if I can't, then I don't mind going back to slavery.'

AC: For all of us, we come to some position of autonomy after working our butts off for years and years. It has taken you eleven years to now say, 'Let's not shoot for a year; let's wait till this script is in place.' But it's going to take everybody here a while to get there, right? So, when you are in a position where you can't call the shots, what is it that you focus on to keep going?

KR: To be honest, it is not going to be that difficult if you can't call the shots. It's not that you feel, 'Oh my God! I want to take control or I want to take charge.' It's only when you start to realize that your brand is so big that it is bigger than the film, and the director and the producer. The only person who is getting bashed is you! That's when you feel, 'I didn't take any of these decisions.' Then there is no one you can complain to because the one who is getting all the gaali and joota (abuses) is you, and the one whose brand is coming down is yours. That's when you begin to realize that if you did not take the call, too bad for you. Why didn't you? You can't keep going to your mamma and papa.

When I was a relatively smaller actor during *Fashion* or *Metro*, it was a glorious time for me. You go to the sets, do your bit, the film is a flop, but you still keep getting jobs. I don't think that the time was suffocating. It only got worse when my name became bigger than the film; then it became a bit of a tricky business. Before that, it was not.

Like when I was doing *Once upon a Time in Mumbai*, I had a good time. I didn't have to worry about its fate. During that film I was getting a half-an-hour job. You get a lot of jobs because you are good at what you do. You are an actor at that time and keep getting jobs because you are good. All my films failed and even then I would get jobs, but it gets tricky when there is a bit of... of stardom...then it's just about you. Yes, that part is difficult. You come to that point after a very long time, and by then, you understand a lot. You can help it, so every stage has its challenges, but you get a lot of help automatically with your experiences. So it will all work out in the end.

AC: It is not easy; it looks glamorous, but it is not easy.
KR: Yes.

AC: Okay, I am going to ask you to talk about the two scenes that we have picked. These are the two scenes that I absolutely love. The first one is, of course, the wonderful Datto. Let's watch it...
[A scene from *Tanu Weds Manu Returns*, a film where Kangana plays two identical-looking characters, is shown.]

AC: Tell me about playing two very different women and acting against yourself.
KR: It's gratifying on another level because in a script the actor's arc is one, and it gives you a lot of hold on it. But if you have two arcs in the script, it's like living two lives simultaneously. Sometimes acting can be done with very easy tricks, with easy approaches. For example, if I was doing these two characters, their body language is an important aspect of it. Just have one word for a character, give it to that character, rather than having an entire arc of that character.

When you are trying to perform a scene, you can't have, no matter how many notes you made, all that baggage and go to the sets when you are performing. So, I suggest you all have an easy approach...you need to think, 'How do I make it a bit different from the conventional?' Tanu is a girl from Delhi University...she is a flirt who gets a lot of attention from men. So what would be the conventional body language for her? Someone who is very flamboyant, right? That's what you would think. But I made her extremely anxious, extremely vulnerable, and very insecure.

And then there is another character you have: Datto. So, what are her characteristics that the writer has given me? She has buck teeth. So she must have been embarrassed about it while growing up, she has a complex. She is very young. Her parents have abandoned her, so she lives with her bade bhaiyya (older brother) and he loves her because she is a bright kid. She has a lot of pressure on her.

So I feel she is a sensitive person, she is someone who is extremely intuitive about others' feelings; she is a really nice girl. So, what would be the body language for her? It is going to be conventional, and I will make her too good to be true...holier than thou. That person will be very timid, very obedient, very sincere in her body language. My problem is, I don't like retakes, I can't do more than two takes with the same sort of emotions. Then I just have to take a half-an-hour break to arouse myself to the same set of emotions.

AC: What happens? Do you get tired?

KR: Yes, I get emotionally exhausted. So if I have done the whole monologue of Datto, maybe twice, maybe there was a track, there was a camera. Then I go with Tanu's character in the van and I do this. Then again I go back, as I am doing two characters. If there is too much chaos in your mind then you forget both arcs.

So I told Aanand ji (Aanand L. Rai) that I will give two takes each, and he was okay with that. He did a lot of rehearsals, and the best part was that he did take only two takes each. That's the thing about collaborative directors—they do understand, they never question why or why not because eventually you too want to give your best.

But sometimes actors don't have a showroom or a machine; they work through their bodies, and it's very limited. You are limiting things, not using your mind. Writers work through their minds but actors work through their bodies, and it's very limiting. That's why it's the least favourite of my jobs, because after a while, you get exhausted. Like when I did a scene, I was in my car post pack up, you do not know where you belong, because there are so many arcs in your own personality.

That's why I feel actors are great people, because they have so many parallel lives, and they still manage to maintain their sanity. That's why, for me, I just take one word for one character rather than having a world of arcs; just one word, such as anguish, or for a character such as Julia who is needy, she is simply needy, so sometimes one just takes the easier route.

AC: That's the one 'sur' (musical note).

KR: Yes, just one 'sur', and then, after that, you do the scene. It helps in your body language. It is an easier technique. It's not my technique; it is someone else's, but when I heard about it, I said this is the best thing to tell someone who is starting out, rather than using big words. Later on, you will figure out what your technique is, but, to begin with, just one word. If you are playing Datto, it's 'swag' and if you are playing Tanu, then 'emotionally fragile', just two words...

AC: Let's say you have done a scene like this. You are completely emotionally depleted, you get into the car, and you are going back home. How do you make yourself switch off so that you can actually replenish for the next day?

KR: It's very hard. When you shoot a film, it's hard, but it's extremely exhilarating also, because all the scenes are not emotionally depleting. Sometimes a character can give you catharsis and a high of extraordinary proportions. So it is party time. I remember when I finished Julia, and Vishal sir messaged me saying how much fun he had, and now he has to go back to the lameness of reality. It was so much fun, so nice being in World War II, I miss the troupe of the forties, the actors, and film cameras and so many things you are exposed to. It is a lot of fun, but there are a few scenes that can take a lot out of you.

AC: Let's take a look at Julia.
[A clip from the film, *Rangoon*, where Kangana's character, Julia, dances and falls on her butt!]

AC: Fabulous! In my mind, Kangana, this is one of the great performances of the year, and if there is any justice at the film awards, which we know there isn't, you would get all the awards.
KR: Thank you, Anu, you are so kind.

AC: No, really, what I liked about you is, you are so vulnerable and so needy, but you are not afraid to be silly. How many actors would be willing to fall on their arse in a scene like this? How did you create her?
KR: The most important thing for an actor is to know that nothing is above the script. And that is the story, and the day, the minute, one realizes that, they have the sense of the higher purpose that we all are working for—the script. So what does the script need—what emotion needs to come out of the scene at that point of time is very important. And when you work towards that, a certain sincerity, a certain graph itself takes you there. My motive here is to give whatever the script needs, and if at all I want to enjoy my vanity, it should be that I will give my script the best it can get by a performer. You are a slave to the script.

So, right now, here, the idea of the script is that this girl and the Japanese soldiers find some sort of compatibility or some sort of friendship while she is captured by them, which Vishal sir, along with his writer, had in mind. This was a wonderfully written scene, and as a performer, my duty was to give my director that performance. When you sincerely work towards that, to give the script that, and given that the Japanese soldiers didn't kill her... she is a character.

AC: I loved it where she is putting his gun down.
KR: Otherwise she would have been shot there, if she didn't justify why they shouldn't shoot her. So you got to justify your script.

You are so shit scared. I mean, look at her, she is like a shivering little mouse. Why would anyone kill someone who is already dead? So, that was the idea—that I should not be threatening or intimidating...and the lines were great too. I try to entertain them, so all of this is a sincere belief that my life is in danger...

AC: So, Kangana, you put in all this work and then a film like this doesn't work. You said that when it didn't do well, you actually felt powerless because people appreciated your performance so much, but not the film. What do you do when that happens? How do you come to terms with it? How do you move on?

KR: It's a bit of a setback, there is no denying it. It's a failure like any other. As much as you would like to look away and be philosophical about it, you realize that it starts to reflect on so many things. How your brand is affected, how your other financial parts are affected, the business gets affected. You can't be philosophical about it! No matter how much you think about the Gita and think that a shloka would work, nothing works. So, you should have it in you to go out there and make sure that you survive, because failures and setbacks are the same everywhere. They will throw you back, and then you have to get up and start again. I don't want to be traumatized by it.

AC: It's hard?
KR: It is hard.

AC: Are there any rituals you follow to stop wallowing and just move on?
KR: Well, the biggest jolt is to your confidence, to your craft and the honesty of your craft. You think I am going to do my work properly come what may; I am going to fight for it; I am going to make sure that I am on time and I am convinced that I am going to go all out. I am not going to attend my birthday. I am going to sacrifice everything...cancel the date I have with my lover...f**k him if he is leaving...I am going to believe...

AC: This is my mission...
KR: This is my mission and this is what is according to the universal law of karma. This is the right thing to do, and eventually, you find out it isn't! You don't know what is! Maybe I could have gone on that date and had a birthday party and come back late, and not worked with so much of conviction. I didn't fight for that damn line with my director which anyway got cut at the editing table. It all feels shit. But that's all a part of life, and yes, I think time heals everything. If your film flopped in February, you feel like shit in March, but by August, September, it doesn't hurt that much.

AC: I read a column that Barkha Dutt had written about you, where she said that what she really likes about you is the fact that you are not afraid to be disliked. She says you embrace your unpopularity. Is that true?
KR: Well, honestly, I would like to be liked, but it's just that when it's not the way I would like it to be, I don't mind the other way. But it is not that I go out there thinking who cares whether you like me or not. Why would I come here if I didn't care about it in the first place? But yes, I wouldn't be fussing about it. For me, it's not something that is going to affect me as an individual. It's not so important, how people like to paint a picture of themselves in an environment. I will not. I would be exhausted to do that for someone to like me. How people like to have fans by giving a picture of their lives, their families or having a vacation.

AC: Like constructing a whole narrative.
KR: Yes, like the food is placed in a way that looks too good to be true. I can't make that much effort, but I am putting an effort as you can see, and I definitely would like you all to like me.

AC: You know, Kangana, you have been instrumental in altering the narrative around women in Hindi cinema. I think you and several of the others...
KR: You know, I have an analogy. I have been a victim of this

shift. This shift was anyway coming, and our generation has seen a paradigm shift. Be it mobile, network, digital, online, internet—so the world has become this one place, and it is not injustice against women; there are a lot of rights, there are a lot of things that are coming out. Like there is a problem there, or this is not right or there is a loophole in the system. People have been discussing that on a sort of world platform, and I think it was anyway coming, but I have become a victim of this shift.

AC: Why victim?
KR: Victim, because like a blast happens and a person falls on stage and wonders, am I here? Oh, she is the one who defused the bomb? I am, like, okay (*laughing*). Okay, fine then.

AC: Kangana, but you are extremely vocal about what you want. You haven't been shy about expressing what you want, and the things that you see as necessary to be an actor...
KR: Well, I would suggest that a lot of women are like that.

AC: Of course.
KR: One shouldn't discredit them. Some of them are amazing. But I won't take the credit away from myself. My story is most definitely an unusual one, but the shift was anyway going to happen. I am glad...jokes apart...I am glad to be the catalyst if I can call myself that, not the pioneer, but a catalyst. I will settle for that.

AC: Sometimes when I see the things around you in the media, and as someone who has been at the frontlines, applauding as you have soared, I am afraid for you.
KR: I know (*laughing*).

AC: I want to see this continue to grow; you are going to be a director next. Do you ever feel afraid for yourself?
KR: Yes, I do sometimes. I do feel afraid for myself, but right now, I don't have those many fears because I do feel to an extent that I have accomplished a lot. I have built a house in Manali; it is

a beautiful house. I have not seen anything more beautiful than that in my life, and I tell myself if nothing works I can always go back there. Somewhere you need to draw the line; you can't go all the way every time.

There are things, right and wrong, and I have all my life to live the way I want to. So I say what I say, and somewhere at the back of my mind, even if people want to prove me a liar, sometimes as mad, sometimes a witch, a whore, whatever is in store for me, I tell myself, 'You tried. If you win, you continue, if you lose, you go back to Manali and write your book and enjoy the snow, the bonfire.' It's a beautiful life, so either way, I am going to be okay.

AC: You are sorted.
KR: Yes, I am sorted.

AC: Tell me about *Teju*.
[To the audience] That's the film she is going to be directing. What do you think is the most important quality for a director to have?
KR: The most important quality for a director to have is to believe in magic.

AC: What do you mean?
KR: To believe in the miracle or the mystery of life. When a person, especially a creative person, starts to become a technician, he or she starts to believe too much in the technique of it and forgets the magic. I think it is very important to do your writing in the morning. Have your script ready, have everything set up for that script, be completely prepared, but surrender just before you get to the set. Surrender to something even more beautiful, to be in the hands of someone else who would want to communicate through you.

The greatest film I have seen that has had the theme in the centre is *Avatar*. It's a beautiful film about space but the story within is so childlike, it seems like a stupid story to have. And *Interstellar*, with space being the backdrop, and science. And it is just a father-daughter story which is about love. That too so karmic in nature, so spiritual, that you feel that the juxtaposition of these two worlds is so beautiful.

I think *Interstellar* without the soul, is such a rubbish film. What is most important for a director is to continue to believe in the magic of human existence. You can make a small film, but it has to have the magic.

AC: That's lovely. Kangana, thank you so much, it has been such a pleasure.

On Bold and Unusual Choices

*Varun Dhawan, Anushka Sharma,
Sriram Raghavan and Navdeep Singh*

Film Companion brought its first 'Adda' session, a space where people from the film industry put their hair down and have a candid discussion about cinema, with Anushka Sharma and Varun Dhawan, and directors, Sriram Raghavan (*Badlapur*) and Navdeep Singh (*NH10*).

In 2015, Sriram's *Badlapur* and Navdeep's *NH10* released within a few weeks of each other. They were not your usual commercial films, but starred Hindi cinema's biggest young stars, Anushka and Varun.

Those are two important films that showed how the younger generation of actors is willing to experiment with roles, and has no problems taking on 'dark roles' if they spell success. Anushka Sharma and Varun Dhawan speak about their work in *NH10* and *Badlapur* respectively, and why they did these films. In fact, they fight to prove that there's nothing dark or offbeat about their latest choices.

♥

AC: Thank you for being here for the first *Film Companion* 'Adda'. You guys watching need to know that it's taken me months to get these people into the room but...
AS: Only because of Navdeep and Sriram.
AC: That's right, not because of you two.
VD: Too starry, man.
AS: Yeah, we kept changing our dates to get these guys to come here.
VD: So much ego!
NS: Because we actually had some work.

AC: So, look, the vibe I am aiming for is exactly this. We just bumped into each other on the street and now we are sitting here, having coffee, which is actually water in the mugs, and talking movies. First of all, congratulations to you two (Varun and Sriram)! I enjoyed both the movies so much, and *Badlapur* has the second highest opening of the year.

How amazing is that! You guys are walking with a little spring in your step?
VD: Not at all, actually. It's so weird that two days before the movie released, I was thinking, box office is going to happen and all. But I remember Sriram coming to me and telling me, 'Hey, Varun, don't worry about the money. I'm happy with your performance and let Dinu (Dinesh Vijan) worry about all this. And Dinu was just sitting like that, feeling very lonely.

And then my co-actor Nawaz (Nawazuddin Siddiqui) also told me the same thing, *'Paisa-vaisa toh chalta hai, hum logon ne cinema kiya hai yaar* (Money comes and goes, we have made good cinema).'
AS: But after a point, what can directors and actors do anyway? It's like you've done it and after that you can't be saying, *'Abhi teen lakh aur kamane ke liye mujhe voh kar lena chahiye tha* (To earn three lakhs more, I should have done that).'
VD: No, you can't, but I guess because of the previous films I've

done and because I am going and dancing to 'Jee Karda'...I made Nawaz also dance to promote this film. I mean, I've done crazy, weird stuff.

SR: He's done some mad things.

AS: During promotion, not in the song?

VD: No, no, no, in the promotions. So, in my heart I was thinking, 'Dude, I've really gone all out for this movie and I tried to make people feel the passion and stuff like that, which we all do, I guess.'

AS: But I think that's very important, because you are a commercial actor. You're doing a film which is considered offbeat, not really mainstream. So I think you must use your stardom to promote films like these.

SR: Yeah correct, absolutely correct.

AS: Because, ultimately, it would be nice if more people are watching this.

VD: I saw something that she did lately, which caught my eye. You did that hitting scene with the selfie stick?

AS: Yeah, a rod.

VD: So I think, even with promotions, as actors we need to get more creative and do something new because promotions have become quite boring.

AC: But are you two (Anushka and Navdeep) breathing a little easier, because if a film like *Badlapur* gets an audience like this then you know that there is an audience for grimmer, tougher stories?

AS: Absolutely. I was very, very happy when I heard that.

I saw it in the theatre (and I have spoken to Varun about it). So, I saw the reaction there and it was instant. It was very reassuring.

NS: And it paves the way for you, so it's great to see movies like this.

VD: The good thing that is happening with these movies is that people are not saying, 'Oh I want to watch this star, or I want to watch this person.' They are saying, 'I want to watch this movie,' which has not been happening lately. So, I think films need to be given importance, they need to be bigger than the actors, the directors, the producers, everyone. I think what went right with *Badlapur* in the marketing was that we did commercialize the product more than, sorry (to Sriram) not the product, sorry, the film.

AC: (*laughs*) Talking like a true mainstream star.

VD: We did commercialize the film more than what it was, to make it appealing to a larger audience.

NS: And I think that's really important to get the audience in, because a lot of people get in like that, but just to get them in is the trick.

AC: So how do you (Varun and Sriram) guys do it?

VD: First, these films need to be marketed.

AS: And not like a template.

AC: Exactly.

VD: *Voh toh maza nahi aayega* (Then it won't be fun).

AS: People have to get very creative with such films. That's why you need good marketing teams to come up with some different kinds of plans. Otherwise, they follow a set template and I've done that with so many of my films, you just do the same thing.

VD: What do you usually do?

AS: You go to these shows, visit malls...

VD: Do you dance?

AS: No. I did it the first few times and I found it damn strange. I thought, why am I dancing in these spaces such as malls and all? When I was growing up, I didn't think, '*Main aake mall mein naachungi* (I'll come and dance in the malls)?'

SR: He's (Varun) done that. I went with him.

AC: You danced for *Badlapur*?

SR: Yeah, yeah.

VD: Full *nachaniya* (dancer). I'll show a video after this.

SR: He's going all over and I went once just to see the thing. Nawazuddin told me to just come to see what happens. My own thing was, 'Great he's dancing, they'll come and see *Badlapur*'.

AC: But how do you sell *Badlapur* by dancing?

VD: Because it's a different type of dance.

AS: Nobody believes this rubbish.

VD: It's aggressive.

AS: You did an aggressive dance in a mall?

VD: Not in a mall. I did it only in colleges. So what I did was not usually what I do for other films. I've done krumping in 'Jee Karda' and krumping is like a western maatam (mourning), it's like you're hitting yourself.

AS: *Aapne differently marketing kaise kari? Maine us wali ke liye krumping kiya tha, is wali ke liye maine aggressive dance kiya tha* (How did you market it differently? I did krumping for the previous film and for this one, I did an aggressive dance)!

VD: Yeah, I'm serious and it worked for us. And I had this plan in my head.

AC: Really?

VD: I'm not lying about it. I made Nawaz dance.

AC: What helps is creating that excitement when you go to meet people.

VD: Arrey, but if you're out somewhere, and there are 25,000 people or 15,000 people, what are you going to do?

AS: You can't just come in and talk about the film. That's true. You've got to do something like...

VD: You'll recite dialogues from your film?

AS: I say a dialogue, and with girls, I think you just laugh or something and they start...

VD: You just have to say 'Hey guys! How are you?' That's damn unfair, dude. The minute the girl comes, or she waves, says hello or something, the boys just lose it, man.

AC: And you don't get that response?
AS: I feel the most girly at that time.
VD: No, I can't say hey and all—they'll be like, *'Haan, chal na.* (Yeah yeah.)' So, I have my lines. I say it in all my film lines.
AS: You learn it and go, if you're doing promotions.
VD: 'Haan waise mein dikhta hoon sweet, innocent, swamy type ka, lekin actually hoon harami type ka (Actually, I look like a sweet, innocent, harmless type of guy, but I am actually a bastard).' So, for 'Jee Karda', I'd say, *'Main gaana gaaonga, aap log mere saath gaao* (I will sing a song, you guys sing with me).' I say, *'Oh mera jee karda',* and then they all sing *'Mar janeya'.*
AS: Actually, some actors are very good at playing the crowd like that...
VD: You've promoted with Shah Rukh Khan.
AS: Yeah, he is, and Ranveer (Singh) is very good with that. I think I'm not very good in front of crowds.

AC: Anushka, you are, of course, also the producer on this one. Do you think that's the way actresses in Hindi movies or actresses anywhere, I just saw Wild and Reese Witherspoon optioned that book, she sourced that story, she created a role for herself, and that's now an Oscar nominated role, is this the way for women to actually get good roles? First, you find the clout to enable films like this to happen and then you just find the material. Is that the way to do it?
AS: Yeah I guess, I mean, what happened with *NH10* was that it just seemed like a more commercially viable option for me to let go of my actor's fees and just say that, okay, fine. It's easier then for people to put money in a film like this because as much as we say that we know offbeat films and all that, the industry is not lapping it up and picking up these films, like they want to make changes or they want alternate stuff like that, if you know what I mean.
AC: So the stars have changed, the audience has changed, but

the guys signing the cheques have not changed?
AS: They have not changed. So what you have to do is, you need to say, okay fine I'll get involved with you guys in risk-sharing, and then it's okay. Then it's easier to put up these films but I'd rather do that, otherwise you'll be making compromises with the movie by saying, *Accha hum yeh nahi kar sakte, voh nahi kar sakte* (Oh we can't do this, we can't do that). Already we felt like we were not really given that kind of open field to play. That is after I've said okay, fine, let's just produce it, which seems much easier than making a film like this. This is what I felt, and that's why the decision happened.
VD: The one thing I ask myself is why are these films called offbeat? I mean I'm in *Badlapur*, Anushka Sharma is in *NH10*. Why are they called offbeat in the first place? Look at the stories. What is the story of *Badlapur*? It's a revenge story. When did revenge become offbeat?
AS: It's a commercial topic.
VD: In *NH10*, I'm not going to reveal the story, I don't know if you'll want to give that away, but I know that she is hitting a lot of people and she and her husband fall in trouble. So I know you're kicking ass and there's action in the film.
AS: So, when I'm looking at it, I'm thinking this is actually a very, very commercial topic, but people are not looking at it like that because we were told to do songs. We were told, *Lip sync gaana ho sakta hai* (Can you do a lip sync song)? And we said, these guys are about to get into trouble. They get out of the car and start dancing in the khet (field).

AC: *Maarne se pehle ek gaana ho jaye.* (Let's do a song before we start hitting them.)
AS: Yeah. There were suggestions about it like *khet mein ek gaana kar sakte hai* (we can do a song in the field).
AS: And sometimes, when they're making suggestions, they're so convinced about what they're saying, because that is also a reality.

You know what I'm saying?
VD: Yeah, yeah.
AS: So you're almost thinking, *bach gaye*. (I am saved.)
SR: Can I ask you (Anushka) a question?
AS: Yeah.
SR: I often wonder about big stars because if their last film has made ₹130 crores or ₹200 crores or whatever, and if I go to him or her with a much smaller but maybe darker film...if these guys are thinking, okay, I have to make at least 140 now because I made 130 last time, then...
AS: I'll tell you, I know what to say. I'll tell you how I think. Okay. Now *PK*, I did that, I had one commercial film. Even if I do *NH10*, which is not commercial...
VD: Say how much did *PK* make?
AS: A lot of money.
VD: Say it aloud.
AS: I don't know, it's ₹300 crore or something.

AC: ₹330 crore.
AS: So I think, I can't compare this film to the last film. I can't say, *PK ke jitna yeh karna chahiye, maine utna kiya toh mujhe usse upar karna chahiye* (It has to do as well as *PK*, I have done that so I need to do better). But I'll think like this. *Main PK kar rahi hoon, main ek Bombay Velvet kar rahi hoon* (I am doing a *PK* and I am doing a *Bombay Velvet*), so I'm secure as a commercial actor. So, if I do a *NH10*, we go all out and do it for the film, for what the story is. I'll handle my career like that.
VD: That's very right.
AS: And that's the way I want to see it in the future also. I guess, maybe do you (Varun) think that happens a little bit more with male actors where they have to be constantly breaking box office records on their own?
VD: Male actors are very insecure, man.
AS: Not insecure. This is what is expected of them, every time.

Their last film se upar (more than their previous film).
SR: That's what I am worried about.
VD: That's by the trade. Why do we compare Shah Rukh and Salman Khan? Why should we compare them? Why are they supposed to be compared?
AC: But Varun, I really think that to some extent, for the men, they have become trapped in this 100, 200, 300 crores thing because if you look at the films that they did last year, it's just more of the same.
VD: So the idea is to never do a 100-crore film. *Kuchh bhi kar lo* (Do whatever you have to).
AC: That's right. *Mera plan yeh hai* (That's my plan).
VD: *Main idhar neeche mein khelunga* (I will play at a lower field).
AS: Because it's not fair to compare a *Badlapur* to a full, *seven dancing wale gaane* (with seven dance numbers) kind of a mainstream film. It's not fair.
VD: Yeah, yeah.
AS: If that's the way an actor's success is being judged then we need to do something about it. Right?
AC: Yeah. What's amazing is the two of them (Sriram and Navdeep) worked together in 2007, their last film, *Johnny Gaddaar* and *Manorama Six Feet Under* released within a week of each other.
AS: What?
AC: Yes.
SR: Yeah.
VD: That's pretty, pretty cool.
AS: Oh my God. That's awesome.
NS: That wasn't the plan but I was supposed to do this movie called *Basra*.
SR: The thing that happened was, we didn't get an audience at that time. I mean, the films were both liked, but one week, two

weeks, they were out of the hall. In the second week also, it got some odd shows and so on, but I think today it's a little better.

AC: That's what I was going to ask you. What has changed? Was it easier to get these movies made? Was it easier to get these guys to sign on? Did the money men write the cheques easier?
NS: I think actors are more open to...stars are more open, let's call them that, to doing different films. I think the younger stars, the kind of films they watch, they want to sort of participate in that kind of thing. That's definitely changed. I think even the audience is changing. I don't know whether it's true, but a lot of people watch TV now. We used to watch *Dexter* and things like that and then they want to see people they identify with.
VD: The funny thing is, when I sat down to do the movie, he (Sriram) did not believe me. He tested me.
AS: How?
VD: I don't know why you didn't believe me when I told you.
SR: No, no, my worry was after a few days, because I know his circle and his dad is my senior in the institute (FTII, Pune), they're going to advise him not to do it eventually. And I had another story, I remember, which was much more fun. It's a thriller also. And I said, 'Are you sure you're going to do this one over that?'
VD: *Yeh bhi hai, yeh bhi hai mere paas* (I have this, I have that too.).
SR: Matlab (I mean) I thought he'd back out at some point.
AS: But I think this happens because...didn't you (Navdeep) say that you told Vikram (Vikramaditya Motwane) *jab Anushka ko bolne ke liye pehli baar ki voh nahi karegi, voh nahi karegi* (when he wanted to approach Anushka, you said that she won't do it)?
NS: Haan (yes), we were sort of skeptical, and like arrey why waste two-three months chasing someone, yaar, let's go straight down...
AS: The strange thing is that I think, as actors, when we get this, it is pretty awesome. You just need to communicate, guys...
VD: You know what I think? The one thing about the newer

generation is that they don't latkao directors (leave them hanging).
AS: That is absolutely true.

AC: You say yes or no?
VD: Yes, they say yes or no.
AS: Yes, yes absolutely. Because I find it damn strange when they say, 'Will you tell us in a week or two?' I'm like, 'No, I'll tell you in four days.'
VD: Exactly.
AS: I guess that happens, because I'm sure they've experienced it before, but I think maybe we're just becoming a lot more respectful of... I don't think actors are like, '*Hum time lenge* (We will take time).' I don't think that works anymore.

AC: But for these two (Sriram and Navdeep) to make these films, for him to make *Badlapur*, for him to make *NH10*, it's what comes naturally. You two (Varun and Anushka) come from a more sort of cheerful, sunny, morally uplifting universe of mainstream cinema. So, is there any fear? I mean, Varun, you put yourself against Nawazuddin who I think is one of the best actors in the country. So, are you scared, 'Damn, what if I just can't do it, or what if I get found out, what if I look like a fraud?'
AS: I don't think actors think like, 'This is what I fit into.' In fact, I would like directors who look at me and think that she can fit into anything.
VD: Exactly.
AS: So like today, if I am doing a film like *NH10*, I did *PK*, I am doing *Bombay Velvet*, I'm thinking okay, this is working out, like different directors who make...
VD: Different films.
AS: Because, see, them being different is what an actor needs. So if Navdeep is different and Anurag Kashyap comes from a different background and so does Rajkumar Hirani, I am getting that diversity in my films. So, as an actor you want that, at least I'm looking for that. I want all directors to approach me because

an actor is not supposed to be any particular way. We are supposed to mould ourselves into different...

AC: I know, but that's not how it is here. No?

AS: But now even directors are looking at you differently. When I asked Anurag, because I was so used to people telling me... When I started off, I was getting those kinds of Punjabi roles and stuff like that. I was frustrated, I was like, 'What is this?' I was bored, and by the time I did *Band Baaja Baaraat*, I felt like, I've had it, I can't do this anymore. So, when Anurag came to me with this script, I asked him, 'Are you sure I can do this?' You start doubting yourself. That's what happens if the industry does that to you, but then there will be a person like Anurag who'll come and offer you this film, Navdeep will come and offer you *NH10* and you're back there, you're changing things for yourself.

AC: But is it scary, Varun, to stand in a frame with Nawazuddin?

VD: No. You don't know what's going on in my head when I'm standing with him. And you don't know what's going on in his head when he's standing with me. If you've met Nawaz, he's so down to earth.

AC: Of course, he is.

VD: When the film did well, I made Karan (Johar) speak to him. So, I couldn't stand up, but he was saying, 'Thank you, sir, thank you sir'. He nearly sat down on the ground, and I was saying, '*Nawaz bhai, kya kar rahe ho* (Nawaz bhai, what are you doing)?' He is too chilled out, and in fact he is so sweet and so nice.

AC: He's not intimidating?

VD: Not at all. See, I tell you. My first film was opposite Rishi Kapoor, okay? Then after that I got one with Anupam Kher, I did some scenes. Then I've worked with Ashutosh Rana, so I think all these guys, they are actors, yaar. They don't want to mollycoddle you and say, '*Beta yeh scene hai* (Son, this is the scene)'. I think my advantage is this, that I had an upbringing where I saw Govinda do scenes with Amitabh Bachchan, and I have seen Salman Bhai do scenes with the biggest of the older generation actors and be like Salman, whatever.

AS: I think that's being a bit selfish, but it's not that you need that little babying.

VD: See we are here to do work. Our films are being made in crores, you're trying to entertain people, you can't come in and get intimidated at this stage. Do that during your training, get intimidated during your training, get scared during your training, your workshops.

AS: Or you wouldn't do it, you wouldn't take it. You would say, *Mujhe nahi karna yaar, pura chaar mahina* (I can't do it for four months). I don't want to go, drive myself crazy with my insecurity, so I probably won't do it.

VD: I have this friend, Kavish, who Sriram has met. He's a very good friend of mine, and whenever we see any of these Khans' films or any of these really big stars' films and I tell him, *arrey yaar* this guy was superb in the film, what power. He says *arrey itna toh hona chahiye na* (He should have that much power). I mean, he's been working for so many years. *Actor acting nahi karega to kya karega* (If an actor won't act, then what will they do)?

AC: Correct. So was there a moment when you guys (to Sriram and Navdeep) really wished there was somebody else in your films?

SR: No, for me what happened was before I began shooting; we used to talk a lot. Then I saw *Main Tera Hero* which was released after we had signed him and I had a moment of doubt because there is so much energy and bounce there. I said, how am I going to bottle this, but then, the rest, as you say, was...

VD: I think there are a lot of variations that I like to do as an actor, so the scene where Yami (Gautam) who plays my wife is dying, I went damn loud. I didn't realize...I was doing, 'Misha, Misha, talk to me.' I had a blast doing it. I thought...Oscar!

And there was one doctor also in the room and I was shaking

Misha. Misha would have died if she was not dead yet, I had shaken her so much. And then I heard 'cut', and I was thinking, 'Yami, poor girl, wake up'. I think she was traumatized by what this guy did. This was the beginning of the film—we had just started shooting, and Sriram looked at me and said, 'No, no, no. It can be inside also.' And Anil Mehta also felt the movie might not get made or something.

AC: But when he did this 'Misha, Misha, Misha', did you have a moment of total panic?
SR: Yes, like now we need to talk to this guy. I think it is really hard for actors to do nothing, just stand there. Everything is in your head, your eyes.
VD: I remember a lot of things. I was supposed to open the door and go in. So I opened the door, and I had an umbrella in my hand, so I said I won't open it with my hand, I'll open it with my umbrella. Sriram said, I am just telling you to open the door... just open the door.
AS: Because at that moment you're thinking, what can I do here? I know he's going to pick this up, but how can I make this different?
SR: Exactly.
VD: *Isko thoda entertaining karte hain* (Let's make this a bit interesting). How can I achieve this?
SR: Make it my scene.

AC: I am opening the door, I need to make it mine (*laughs*). Anushka, did you have to unlearn?
AS: I don't know. Now, I wouldn't know, maybe like Navdeep was keeping...
NS: No, no, for us it did not happen like that. We, Anushka, Neil (Bhoopalam), and myself, spent a fair amount of time in workshops and stuff and we pretty much were on the same page before we went in.

AC: So the rhythms were the same?

NS: The rhythms were the same, and just see, we're getting those two together into the same because Neil comes from this theatre background and Anushka comes from this more commercial end of the industry, but we were fine.

AC: So tell me before we wrap. Do you two (Varun and Anushka) think that you are walking away with these films as better actors? Is there something you've learnt through the process of this new environment?

AS: I would think so. Also I feel, somewhere, with a film like *Badlapur* doing well, if *NH10* does well, it is very reassuring, and probably gives me more strength to do more such films. So, just for that, I really wish that the film does well, so that I can continue to do this. And there are naysayers coming and say I told you so, I told you so.

SR: That's true.

AS: So that's the reason why I really, really want the film to do well and I wish that for any actor who's trying to do something differently.

AC: What's the funniest thing somebody said to you guys about why you shouldn't do these films? Like the most outlandish, comical thing that somebody might have said.

VD: Most outlandish, haan (yes), I can tell you what my dad said because he met Huma (Qureshi) on a plane ride and Huma told him ki, 'Arrey, David Sir, I read the script, and what a script, it's damn dark, it's damn dark.' So when Dad came home, I remember, at night, 10:30 or so, I was in the room and he came and said, 'Varun, you signed *Badlapur*?' He did not know I'd signed it. So I said, 'Yeah.' He said, '*Huma mili flight mein, Huma bol rahi thi bahut dark hai*; agar *Huma ko dark lag rahi hai, toh kitni dark hogi* (I met Huma on the flight. Huma told me it's dark. If Huma thinks it is dark, it must be very dark).'

AC: (*Laughs.*) So that's the other level of darkness?

VD: Yeah, he said, *'Kitni dark hai* (How dark is it)?' I said, 'Paa, just relax, just chill.'
SR: I was very sure that he would call me up and say...

AC: *Mera hee beta mila tha* (Did you not find anybody but my son)? And for you, Anushka, did anybody say anything?
AS: Uh, no, not really. Also, I kept quiet about it. I was not talking about it too much because I didn't want to hear all this.

My family didn't know anything, and now, when the trailer came out, everybody was talking about it, everyone was calling me and stuff like that. But before that I didn't know what I would tell them, so I just kept quiet and kept doing it. Also it helped me that *PK* and *Bombay Velvet* were happening at the same time, so people were talking about that. I was saying, *haan theek hai, chalo, hum log aise hee nikaal lenge beech mein.* (Okay, fine. We will just bring this film out in the midst of all this.) When you do such films, it's like a keeda (worm). You do such films, and after that you want to do this. It's a great feeling, that's the whole thing of performing, and it's something else.
VD: What are you (Sriram and Navdeep) all feeling? I don't think your feeling was not what we were feeling.

AC: Directors are just very quiet. Silent.
SR: I actually wanted *Badlapur* to do well because I just felt he is doing such a daring thing and he will just feel discouraged completely if it is rejected completely. Then you say, why do these things? Now that it has done well, he says, I still don't know very well but I think he'll definitely say, next time I'll try something else, and I think actors should be like that.

AC: It enables you.
VD: We are going to announce our next film. It's called *The Dark Lord*.
AS: *The Dark Lord*? L-O-R-D?
VD: L-O-R-D.

AS: It's about a dark lord?

AC: Anurag Kashyap says, 'What is this dark cinema, dark cinema? Is *Gone Girl* called dark cinema?'

VD: Nawaz says the best thing, '*Kyuki main dark hoon, toh isliye aap log bolte ho ki dark film* (Because I am dark, that's why you say it's a dark film).'

SR: Arrey, I had a friend who actually saw it and said, it is dark but it is well lit. He's not from the industry.

AS: *Yeh actually kisi ne kaha tha mere ko ki, 'Tumhara night shoot hai?'*

I said, '*Haan, night shoot hai.*'

'*Poori picture night mein hai? Bahut dark nahi ho jayega?*'

(Someone had asked me this. You have a night shoot?'

I said, 'Yes, it's a night shoot.'

'The whole movie has been shot at night? Won't it be too dark?)

AC: So, directors, are you feeling heartened when stars like them say...

NS: Yes, absolutely, I mean, because that's the only way films like this can get made, because these stars put themselves up on screens, they're taking the risks. You're on the screens, you're taking the risk, it's your name attached to it, and it's fabulous that they are willing to actually take that on and be out there.

AC: Well, more power to all four of you. Go out and make great movies.

AS: Thank you so much. It was fun.

The Prince of Bollywood

Ranbir Kapoor

When we met Ranbir Kapoor for *FC Unfiltered* before the release of *Sanju*, we decided to discuss everything apart from the movie because it was a conflict of interest for me. Instead, Ranbir and I spoke about a range of subjects—from using a perfume to get into character, giving over seventy takes for *Saawariya*, to why *Jagga Jasoos* failed—with an audience full of film aspirants.

Ranbir and I also chatted about the highs and lows of his career, acting techniques, surviving failure as well as his father Rishi Kapoor's harsh critique of his movies. He told us how he quit smoking, the importance of sacrifice, what he's like when he's in love and how his complex love life enhances his craft!

AC: This is an awkward situation. You are here to promote Sanju and I can't actually talk about the film. It is a conflict of interest because my husband is a co-producer. But we have this amazing audience of film students, film lovers, and acting students, and I thought we could use this opportunity to talk about acting.

RK: Absolutely. I can't say the word 'done', but I am tired of talking about *Sanju*. When we do a film, there is a marketing period, where you're really trying to sell the film to people, trying to take it to the audience. And it's the most tiring process ever. You might do films such as *Gandhi* and *The Last of the Mohicans* and they might tire you as an actor, but those five days of promotions can kill you. So, I am very happy not talking about *Sanju*.

AC: Deepika (Padukone) always tells me, 'Don't ask me about my acting process. I don't want to talk about it.' Can you articulate it? Can you tell us how you transform into other people? Are there any rituals that you follow?

RK: Yes, of course. I would like to share my experiences, or my techniques or my method, whatever you call it. What happens is, every film comes with its own character, its own method. There is a new set of procedures you have to follow. And most of the time, I forget, so if you can remind me, I'd love to share some stuff.

AC: You mean you forget the process you followed.

RK: That's your old you. You're constantly evolving, trying to better your old self, your craft, and your skill. But then again, if you become too skilled, it gets boring. Then you start becoming repetitive. If you have one fixed method for every film, you just start repeating the same nuances and beats that you have already set in your head.

AC: Let's talk about *Jagga Jasoos*. I thought you were so lovely in the movie and it broke my heart that it didn't find more takers. How did you create that guy?

RK: It broke my heart as well, and my bank (account). Anurag Basu belongs to a very different species of directors. When we were working on *Barfi*, there were many times when Priyanka (Chopra), Ileana (D' Cruz), Saurabh (Shukla) sir, and other actors would sit waiting for his shot because we had no idea what was going on. There was no script, no blueprint of where the story was going, though we all knew what the story was. There was no screenplay, so to speak. And dada always improvised, always created. And the good experience we had in *Barfi* lent itself to the making of *Jagga Jasoos*.

It was a very…I can't say complicated character, because it was very simple, very basic. But there were a lot of complications behind it to make it look that simple. I think we had taken too much on our plate. Firstly, it is a detective film. The character stammers, it's a musical, he's finding his father, there's a love story, and it is episodic.

So, it was very hard. Also, I am not good with dialogues. So, I was very happy to work in *Barfi* because I didn't have to say anything. I was talking less. I did not have to memorize lines, which was great. I think the challenge in *Jagga Jasoos* was also not to make the stammer irritating. And also, when you sing, the songs were meant to be said like a dialogue. So, it's not as if you're performing a song in a surrealistic space. It's very real.

AC: You say it takes a lot of complicated things to make it look real. I have felt that about you always. I remember watching *Saawariya* and you just lit up the frame, as dark as that film was. And the surprising part is that I never see you acting, which is what makes you so amazing.

RK: Thank you.

AC: What is the complication that goes behind the scene? I know it's like asking a magician to reveal his tricks.

RK: To be honest, what you finally see on screen is the magic of cinema. But there are so many people behind trying to get your character come to life. My method or my process was very basic from my very first film. I always follow two things. One is to marry the director's mind. It's very important because I am that Bandra boy who has lived a very luxurious life, travelled around the world. But I don't know my own country, my own people, and my own characters. So, I always have to steal their personalities and their experiences for me to be better.

And then there's the love story between me and the director which is also very important. He has to fall deeply in love with me and I have to be deeply in love with him. And then comes that trust that's formed, and then you want to do your best, give yourself to this guy. And that guy is giving and taking more at the same time. That is an amazing relationship you form for those six to eight months of the shoot.

The second thing I have realized is that one has to understand the text and what's written. We see a scene superficially, and from the outside, but there are so many things the writer and the director go through, creating every beat, every line that one says, what the other person says. How does one add a sense of truth to everything? So, I guess, once you know this space, the director's love and you understand the text, your job becomes easy.

But the love story in the beginning and courting the director is harder than courting a woman. It's hard because there are two people who are trying to come together to create something beautiful out of a mess. And it's not like you're going to befriend him for life. It's just for this project. But I really enjoy that because that's where it all starts. I also do stupid superficial things like using a particular perfume for a particular character.

AC: You do that? Vidya Balan said she does it too.
RK: She does that? Great. I am in good company then! But, of course, I don't use the same perfumes she uses! My sense of smell is very strong. And any sensation, any sense, smell, or feel that reminds me of that character helps. What happens is, sometimes you are doing two films at a time, like I was doing *Wake Up Sid* and *Ajab Prem ki Ghazab Kahani* simultaneously. I was shooting for ten days here and then twelve days there and then coming back for ten days here. And there was always an overlap of two days between the two characters. Then, the perfumes began to help me. I had one perfume for *Wake Up Sid* and another one

for *Ajab Prem Ki Ghazab Kahani*.
So, perfume is one thing, shoes are another. I like particular shoes for different characters. This is all pseudo-intellectual stuff; we are not saving the world. We are just trying to make ourselves believe that '*Haan, hum yeh sab preparation kar rahe hain.*' (Yes, we are making all these preparations.) Once you know that, it is just your presence of mind on the set, trying not to come with set notions.

AC: Can you instinctively tell, while you're performing, that a shot is not authentic enough?

RK: I stopped looking at myself at the monitor because I found I was cringing a lot, and I started becoming quite aware of myself. I have realized in these last ten years and the fourteen-fifteen films that I have done, that whenever I have gone home and said, '*Aaj maine kamaal ka shot diya*' (I gave an amazing shot today) that's never good. When I have come home in confusion, unable to understand what I did that day, only then do I start to rethink about the shot I gave for a particular scene and that tomorrow, I have to do something else. That confusing state is really about thriving as an actor. That state has always given me better results than the confidence you come home with.

AC: You said that creative energy comes from isolation, nature and sacrifice. What did you mean by it?

RK: I think isolation is very important for every human being, every actor. It's very important that you love yourself. You don't need another person to be happy and you don't need another person to feel alive. In isolation, you go deeper within yourself, understand certain things. What was the second thing I said?

AC: Nature.

RK: As an actor, you are just consuming nature. You can take in nature. That's the world that will be represented through you. So nature is something that is very important. It keeps me peaceful, balanced and helps me understand my value in this big universe. The third thing is sacrifice. This I learnt from Mr Sanjay Leela Bhansali. He has instilled this value in me that you need to sacrifice a certain amount of personal life and fun that stardom gives you because it will take away from a certain 'believability' and the deep empathy you will feel for your characters. It may sound a bit strange, but that sacrifice holds a great value in my life.

AC: Can you put your finger on what you have sacrificed?
RK: I have sacrificed a lot of friendships. My school gang, for example. I meet them perhaps once a month, while they meet each other maybe three or four times a week. I go there and I am lost in the midst of the conversation. There are new beats of laughter that they have which I don't. I don't want to sound like a crybaby, that I have sacrificed one thing to achieve the other, but I have only sacrificed because I have benefitted from it. So, it is out of choice. It is not because life has given me no other option.

AC: I was chatting with Aamir (Khan) and he said he could consistently choose great narratives because he looked at a project as a producer and not just as an actor. So he saw the whole project and not just his part in it. If that is the case, can we perhaps assume you made some really terrible choices because you were too focused on your part?
RK: Maybe. But you know, since my first film, *Saawariya*, and every film I have made since then, every choice has been mine. I am responsible for every successful film and I am responsible for every failure that I have had. I can't take a third perspective on a script—Do you like it? Should I do it? Will it do well commercially? If I am not connected to the material or the character, I will not be able to do anything about it. I won't be good.

I don't have the skill set that Aamir sir has. That is why he is who he is today. I guess that is something you develop with experience, doing a lot of work over the years, and begin understanding your audience. And I am okay with it. I don't think

Bombay Velvet, Jagga Jasoos, Barfi, Wake Up Sid, or *Rocket Singh: Salesman of the Year,* were experimental films. I thought these were commercial films, because I liked them. I thought, here is a character, a world that I can do something with.

AC: But these are also worthy experiments. I am talking more along the lines of *Besharam*.

RK: *Besharam* was the only film in my career that was by design. I wanted to do this masala film. I don't say masala in a negative way. Masala means a large audience will see and enjoy your film. It's the hardest genre. You can make a nice story like a *Wake Up Sid* or a *Rocket Singh: Salesman of the Year*, and there are very few chances of you going wrong. You may go wrong commercially but there will be a large section of the audience that will like your film. However, to get the extent of love of, say, a *3 Idiots* or a *Bajrangi Bhaijaan* or all the great superhits of Indian cinema like *Dilwale Dulhania Le Jayenge* or *Hum Aapke Hain Koun..!* is the hardest. And sometimes that comes out of the blue. Like Mr Shah Rukh Khan used to tell me that he never saw the potential in *DDLJ*. He always thought it was a silly love story, but see what the film did.

AC: It's still running.

RK: When I did *Rocket Singh: Salesman of the Year*, I thought this is my *Munnabhai MBBS*, and I am set for life. When I did *Ajab Prem ki Ghazab Kahani*, I thought I was screwed. I thought no one will offer me movies anymore, and my career as an actor was over. I didn't have the formula.

AC: So no one knows anything.

RK: No. No one knows. That's the magic of the movies. If everybody knew that, then everybody would be the Khans. But we are clearly not.

AC: You said the next few years are going to be spent entertaining the audience and not proving your acting chops. Are these two necessarily different things?

RK: For me, yes. Let me explain. When I do a film like *Tamasha* or *Jagga Jasoos*, I am also looking at my character, Ved, or Jagga, and what I can do through these characters without necessarily looking at the larger picture. One needs to look at the extreme big picture like Aamir sir said, and understand the value of one's film. Who is the film talking to? What is the budget of the film? How much money are you taking? All of that.

Filmmaking is an expensive medium. You can't do this solely because it is your passion project that's only for yourself. And that's a great lesson I learnt from Raju sir. He has this deep desire to entertain the audience. He neither wants to bore them nor force moral opinions. His film may have moral value and you can take what you want from it, but he wants to entertain you, make you laugh and cry. And he just makes you understand that you shouldn't take life so seriously—you're not saving the world. You're only acting in movies, it is just entertainment. Once you realize that, accept that, then your choices also change. Then it becomes not just about yourself, but about the film as well.

I am still striving. Today I am doing a Raj Kumar Hirani film, but I didn't choose that film, Hirani chose me. Anybody will do a Hirani film, so if *Sanju* is a big success, I couldn't really take credit for it like it's my choice. But if *Jagga Jasoos* was a big commercial success then maybe I could have taken credit for it. Alas, it was not!

AC: I was once talking to a director who said that the problem is that you're the prince of Bollywood. That you're eventually Rishi Kapoor's son and therefore, perhaps you aren't hungry in the same way as Ranveer Singh is. So, perhaps you won't do a two-hero film. Is that right?

RK: Absolutely not. Yes, I do have the luxury of not having to work to feed myself or put a roof over my head, but I have been extremely passionate about the movies. Since I am born into a film family, the perception of my hard work and success is taken away from me, because they say, 'Oh, he got it easy.' Yes, I did get it easy, I agree. But I have worked really hard these past ten years, given myself wholeheartedly to every role that I have done and haven't taken my roles for granted. I have never taken anything I have done in my field for granted. So, there is definitely a hunger in me. This two-three-four hero film doesn't matter. I did a film called *Rajneeti* that had so many heroes. So, no, I am not too insecure or too secure that I don't want to do a two-hero film. I haven't been offered a two-hero film that I have liked and the other actor has also liked. Also, when you do a two-hero film, your job is much easier because you are sharing the burden of failure and success with someone. So, I am looking forward to doing one, but I haven't really been offered something that I have liked.

AC: You said you are too insecure to audition. You never audition, right?
RK: I am not that confident about myself, to be honest. And today, I have a body of work and so I don't need to audition. But if you sent me to Hollywood and asked me to audition for some filmmaker, I don't think I would be good at it. I think it's a confidence issue, and now I am spoilt because I am a working professional. Now people have my films to watch, so they can see this guy...if he can deliver or not. But yes, I am shy about auditioning.

AC: But you're Ranbir Kapoor. Why are you low on confidence?
RK: That's my perception, that's my glamour image, that I am so and so.

AC: But you are supremely talented.
RK: I don't think so. I don't regard myself as supremely talented. That's why I have to work hard, because I know my shortcomings. I know where I can be bad and I know where I have been really terrible in a couple of my films, probably where I have given my

80 per cent and not my 100 per cent.

AC: What is a terrible Ranbir Kapoor performance?
RK: Like *Besharam* or *Anjaana Anjaani*.

AC: But *Besharam* was a bad film.
RK: Yes, so that's what I always maintain. That I am only as good as my film. When the director is good, I am good. I don't live in this fool's paradise that it's because of me that a film works. Take a film like *Rockstar*. I only did the work that people liked because of Imtiaz Ali. If you took out Imtiaz Ali from the film and if I directed it, I would be terrible in it because it was his energy that was in me that I was channelizing.

When I go on the sets and sit in my van, doing my make-up and hair, trying to learn my lines, I am confused. I have anxiety issues about whether I'll be able to do the shot well. Will I be able to surprise my director? Will the director take three or four takes? Oh god, he's asking for the sixth take! It's so embarrassing that there are one hundred and fifty people looking down at me. This Ranbir Kapoor is giving eight takes, ten takes? What's wrong with him? So I have all that going on in my mind. It's an everyday process.

It's not that I have the perception of success or that I am a successful actor and life is now easy. As I said, I am not really happy with what I have achieved today; I have a lot more to do. And I think that drive is important. That insecurity creates that drive, that desire. And if that dies, I will die as an actor as well.

AC: What are the most takes you've ever done?
RK: I started with Sanjay Leela Bhansali, and he doesn't do anything less than forty-five takes!

AC: Are you serious?
RK: So, if I turn my head this way (to his left), I'll have to give fifty takes. There was this shot in this so-called 'towel song' ('Jab se tere naina'), where I had to kind of roll back in this chair,

and fall down, and the towel had to fall in a certain way where my leg was showing. And there was one shot where I was lying down and laughing, and I had to get up and sing. And he is very particular about what beat you catch. He's a very musical director. You fall on this beat, you lift your head here, you laugh here... everything is musical. I did some forty-five or fifty takes one day and my back really broke. Out of sympathy, he said, 'Ok, ok...I'll manage, I'll manage!' So I went home. The next morning when I came on the set, he said he hadn't got the scene, so I had to do another seventy takes to get that exact shot right! So I am already coming from that school, and now when someone takes eight to ten takes, it's like nothing.

AC: So there was this lovely interview you did with GQ magazine where you said, 'I'm nothing more than the characters I have played, the books I have read, and the women I have dated.' What did you mean?

RK: Exactly what I said. These are the experiences. Like today. This experience, the energy of all these guys will probably add to my tomorrow. When I interact with them, when I take your questions, I'll take so much to tomorrow's day of work. That's why I've only said books, relationships, or characters, but there's so much that adds up to who you are as a person or as an actor.

AC: Gender parity is one of the big topics today. This is the era of #MeToo and I have to ask you this.

RK: You don't have to if you don't want to. You know that, right?

AC: No, no I have to... Because, after this, he disappears, okay, guys? This is not somebody who is going to do press again until *Brahmastra* releases, which is going to be two years from now. Am I correct?

RK: No, one year...hopefully.

AC: You are doing a film with Luv Ranjan, who is a massively successful director, but his films are really steeped in misogyny.

Do you, as an actor, worry, or think about the images you're putting out there?

RK: How do you pronounce this word...'misogyny', and 'misogynistic'...right? So, I haven't been part of those films...

AC: No, no, of course not.

RK: So, I am working with a director, who, according to you, has made a misogynistic film. But I am quite conscious of the parts I do. If it was a part that was belittling society or belittling something I feel is unfair, I wouldn't do it. I understand the position I am in and I have to be conscious. I have to be aware. I have to represent a certain value system that I want to express. The film with Luv Ranjan is not that.

AC: Good to know. Benedict Cumberbatch recently said that he won't do a project unless he knows what the female actor in the film or the TV series was getting. And he said it's very important that the men in the film industry take a stand to make a film more equitable for women. Do you think this will ever happen in India? Will men in positions of power, like yourself, take these decisions?

RK: I think somebody just has to do it. If one person does it, it's like a domino effect. But the thing is, in our industry, no one ever reveals what they get paid. I guess for income tax purposes. But my contemporaries such as Deepika, Katrina or Priyanka Chopra...I think they are right up there. It's not like they are getting paid lesser than what I am getting paid. There is a perception that an actor gets X amount of crores, and it's just a perception. Today, there is so much awareness of what your market value is. This is one of the few industries that is so market-based. If your films are doing well, you will get the money you deserve, and if your films are not doing well, you won't. But like you were mentioning Benedict's take on this, my take is, somebody just has to do it. If I am in a project, and, say, there is Deepika in it, and she is a bigger star than me, then there has to be equality. She has to get the bigger piece of the pie. But somebody has to do it.

AC: Who will that 'somebody' be?
RK: I don't know. We'll wait and see.

AC: Is there anything that makes you uncomfortable as an actor? Are there boundaries you won't cross?
RK: I don't think so. I have been physically naked when I dropped a towel in my first film.

AC: What else is left to do, right?
RK: You know, being physically naked is not that hard, but being emotionally naked is way harder. You know, like to get attached to a moment, feel real, feel a sense of truth. But yes, there are certain things, like...what's the word..misog...

AC: Misogynist.
RK: ...Misogynistic. There are certain things you have to be aware of. Like who you are and what you are standing up for, because films are a true representation of you as an artist. You have to be aware of what you are standing up for. Your films have to reflect that. So, yes, certain things that I probably believe are instilled in my value system which I wouldn't go against. But beyond that, whatever it takes for me to be good at my job, emotionally, physically, I'll do it all.

AC: Some two years ago, you did this really lovely interview with Rajeev (Masand) and you talked about wanting to have three children. You said, 'I'll do it the right away. Fall in love, deeply, madly and passionately in love.' You seem to fall in love a lot?
You'll agree with me here. Does it complicate the craft ever?
RK: Falling in love? Falling in love is the greatest thing in the world. When you fall in love, everything is great. Water tastes like sherbet, and you seem like Uma Thurman to me...

AC: I love it!
RK: You feel great. So who doesn't want to be in love?

AC: Yes, but what does it do to you as an actor?

RK: It does something to me as a human being and that's who I am. Acting is my profession. If I feel good about myself, or about waking up in the morning, brushing my teeth and going to work, that's because life is great and love makes your life great, right?

AC: So, can you look at your performances and say, 'That was a beautiful moment in my life'?

RK: No, I don't remember what I was feeling on that particular day, but I can say, 'That was a beautiful moment on-screen', because I cannot forget that my entire day was consumed in getting that particular moment on screen right. But I have a bad memory, I don't remember things.

AC: You just put it behind you?

RK: I don't remember myself. Like when I was fifteen, and before, that entire life of mine has been wiped out. I don't remember.

AC: Really?

RK: Yeah...some bizarre thing.

AC: No memories at all?

RK: No memories. I think I was trying to give up smoking and I went to Germany to get these injections in my ears. The nicotine receptors are here (stroking his left ear), and I took the injections. I feel that really messed with my memory. Not in a very dark, intense way but in some way.

AC: Did you quit smoking?
RK: Yes.

AC: So, a little memory loss, and quitting.
RK: Yeah. I mean smoking would kill you rather than a bad memory, right?

AC: Absolutely.

I was with Vinod (Chopra) and Raju when they showed the *Sanju* promo to your dad. And he actually got tears in his eyes.

What does it feel like to have a parent weep because you're so good?

RK: Firstly, he never expresses what he feels about my work.

AC: Yeah, I can't imagine that happens too often.

RK: Never. I have said this before. He usually sees the films three or four days before the release and I am so tense because he is so honest with his opinion. It matters to me, and with him being an actor, and such a fabulous one, he'll always have a good take. A good commercial take or a good artistic take. So when he saw *Rockstar*, he called me and said, '*Woh last scene mein heroine mar gayi thi ki wapas aa gayee* (In that last scene, did the heroine die or come back)?' So, I said no, no, she died. It was her soul that came on stage. And he said, 'Okay, okay, bye', and disconnected the call!

When he saw *Barfi*, he called me again two-three days before the release and said, '*Kya hai ki tu acting vacting theek kar leta hai* (Well, you act decently), but stop doing these arty warty films!' and he disconnected the call! So he's a hard critic to impress. When Raju sir sent the video to me—in a very candid way he had shot it on his phone—it felt great. In the end, apart from the audience, when your parents are proud of your work, it's a good pat on your back. Like something's going right.

AC: But do you ever talk about it? Will he ever tell you in person?
RK: No. Post that video, nothing's ever been mentioned.

AC: Last year was ten years in the movies for you. What do you know now about an actor's life that you wish you could have told your younger self?
RK: I think, if I can call this a journey, it's been a phenomenal one. I would have liked my younger self to discover this journey again because just the discovery of it has been really awesome. I have also grown up in a film family; I know this world, know what success means, what failure means. I know what success

can do to your head and what failure can do to your heart. So, somewhere I was well equipped when I came into this world as a working professional. There's gratitude too. That is something I have learnt in these ten years. To feel immense gratitude for the fact that I am sitting in this chair, in front of all these amazing people, talking about my craft, and my life. And I would like to credit that to myself. Not because I am born with a silver spoon but because I worked really hard to be here and I feel immense gratitude for this field.

AC: Thank you, Ranbir.

Unfinished

Hrithik Roshan

Hrithik Roshan is an actor who has spent his entire life in front of the cameras and is able to combine consummate skill with larger-than-life stardom. This is what enables him to be a quadriplegic Ethan Mascarenhas in *Guzaarish* and the superhero *Krrish*. He has seen staggering highs and back-breaking lows but he has always stayed the course.

In a free-wheeling conversation with me for *Film Companion*, Hrithik Roshan talks about how he embraces failure with as much ferocity as he does his success. The actor tells us how he always knows the fate of his film well before its release. He even talks about how he sometimes stays away from watching films with terrific performances by his contemporaries, especially when he's feeling particularly vulnerable.

HR: Thank you for inviting me, ma'am. So, why are so many people here?

AC: I wonder! Thank you, Hrithik, for making time for this.
HR: My pleasure.

AC: You, Hrithik, have spent your entire life in front of the cameras.

HR: Yes, I have actually.

AC: We saw you first when you were six years old, dancing to a song in *Aasha* in the 1980s.

HR: Yes, I remember that.

AC: By 1986, you had already graduated to more complex speaking parts. In *Bhagwaan Dada*, you had a full substantial role.

HR: Yes, yes...I remember those days. Not a care in the world. I really believed I was the best actor in the world then.

AC: But was acting then a conscious choice? Or was it just a given, that here's this beautiful boy, born into a film family. Of course, he's going to act.

HR: Beautiful! First of all, that word doesn't seem appropriate, because when I was growing up, my father used to call me Lala.

AC: Why?

HR: Because he didn't like the way I looked. I looked very lazy, and I was. I was not into sports. I used to spend my time getting bored. I think he was just compelled to try and use pain as leverage to push me into doing something good in my life. That was his modus operandi, so to speak, but it worked. At that time, I used to feel like the scum of the earth because I was that Lala. Whenever he saw me on the street, and once I was back home, he would say stuff like, 'I thought that was you. You looked like some beggar on the side of the road.'

AC: But why?

HR: Trying to motivate me. There are two ways you can motivate someone. You can either use pain or you can use pleasure. With the kind of life he had lived, the experiences he had, he thought pain would work more. So, 'beautiful' is not a word that could be used to explain why I wanted to be an actor. I think it started off as a fascination. My father was a hero and every son wants to be like his father. At least most sons want to be like their fathers. My father was a hero in films. So I thought, I am supposed to be an actor too.

AC: But your father at that time was struggling to establish himself as an actor. You have spoken often in interviews about seeing your mother cry because there wasn't enough money to buy vegetables or you were thrown out of an apartment because you couldn't pay the rent. So, what were your first impressions of the actor's life? I mean, did these experiences scar you or were you enamoured? Did you like seeing yourself on screen?

HR: No, I don't think it was because I was enamoured. I think it was more a kind of fear.

AC: Fear about what?

HR: Fear about what I was going to do. I had a stutter at that time. I didn't know if I could act. It was more of a kind of fear about what I was going to do. My father didn't have a business which I could just take over. In those days, I used to wake up at 2 a.m. and I remember this one dialogue in some movie. I would practise that dialogue for hours without the stutter. The fear and anxiety just surrounded me.

'I can't do this, but I have to, because what else can I do? What am I going to do in life?' I had to do something. We are all conditioned by society, and by watching our fathers that happiness is very easy. You have to do a few things in life to be happy. You have to work very, very hard to be successful. If you get fame with it, that's great! You have to find a family, a soulmate and settle down and you have to have kids. All these things equal happiness. We have all been conditioned. But it so happens that it is absolutely not true at all.

What is true, according to me, is that you have to be happy first. You have to find your enthusiasm and your passion and find your ways of creating happiness for yourself. Every single day should be a search for growth and to surmount every single problem that comes your way, because the entire day, the entire life is just a collection of problems. Every single day from sunrise to sunset, you are going to face a lot of problems.

You cannot go to sleep, thinking, 'You know, God, I hope I do not have any problems tomorrow. I hope tomorrow goes without any problems.' I mean, that is stupid. It's not going to happen. So, this is what I believe. You have to train your mind and body to be happy first. And the only way you can do that is through discipline and by the right access to the knowledge that you don't have to run after success. Success will be a by-product of your enthusiasm and your passion and your disciplined life where you are actually training yourself to be happy, and not to make money. The money will be a by-product.

Of course, you can do it the hard way, which is the way I was taught—that it's toil, and you should take pride in wearing your bruises. But what is the quest in life? It is to be happy. Are you ever going to be happy looking at your own story and thinking, 'I have been through so much shit in my life'?

AC: But that was then...this clarity you have now. But at that time...
HR: No, no that time was an absolute mess.

AC: In January 1992, you joined Rakesh ji as an assistant director for *Khel*, and then subsequently, you assisted him on several films, *Karan Arjun*, *Koyla* and *King Uncle*. How did being an AD shape you as an actor? What did it do to you?
HR: Well, first of all, it grounds you completely. Knowing how hard the people behind the camera work takes away the fake ego and pride that an actor or a star might attain if he has no knowledge of what happens behind the camera. And it is essential, I think, for every person, for every actor, to know, in some form, what actually happens behind the camera. I remember I was the sixth assistant, so I was completely...

AC: You were hired as the sixth assistant?

HR: I was hired as the sixth assistant and there were times when I was the last to get my turn to take a bath. By the time I got to the bathroom, there was brown water coming out of the tap because we were shooting in some goddamn place in Nairobi, in the jungles. I was like, 'Oh my God! It's brown, dude. This is supposed to make me clean. This is brown. What do I do?'

I remember going on to the set which was very, very close to my father's suite, jumping the wall, looking left and right, diving into my dad's room from the window, going into his loo, taking a bath there and then showing up late on the sets. As an assistant, there was always some work. So, just the travel, staying hungry, just the patience, and wait—waiting for the star when he is having some kind of a...what shall I call it? You know, actors have problems with their hair, something's always wrong with the hair. I am looking at his hair and thinking, 'Hair is fine, dude!'

AC: So are you a better behaved actor because you have been an AD?

HR: No, no! It made me aware. But that's it. In fact, it's worse. Because I know what I am doing. My hair is not right. And at the same time, I know I have been that guy who I hated as an assistant. I know these assistants are thinking that of me now. What do I do? I still need to get my hair right. But at least it makes me aware. Sometimes actors have this notion that the producer and the entire team are taking them for a ride. 99.9 per cent of the time that is not true. And for them, 99.9 per cent of the time, it is true in their heads. So, now, when I have to take a call like this, I better be absolutely sure. Then I can be guilt-free when I say that I need a day off.

AC: Even while you were an AD you were nurturing ambitions of acting. You did your first photo shoot with Dabboo Ratnani in 1994.

HR: Yeah, right.

AC: What I am intrigued about is that your dad, by now, was a successful filmmaker. Why didn't you go to him and say, 'Dad, I want to act?'

HR: My dad has lived a very hard life. So his instincts were of a man who would never compromise. It's something that I learnt, and it's a damn good lesson to learn—to never compromise. You are not here to please people. You're not here to please your son. You're here to be good and strong and do the right thing. Of course, my dad loves me. He is the first person in this world who looked at me and said that I am a star. Not said, but thought that this guy is a star. And he bet his house and his cars; he mortgaged them all for my first film and I didn't even know.

AC: But you couldn't tell him this? You couldn't articulate that you wanted to be an actor?

HR: I always thought that my father would make my first film. I had taken that for granted. And at the same time, there was a tug of war in my head where I wanted to make it on my own and didn't want him to make my first film. I got my photo session done but I didn't tell my dad. Only my mom.

AC: Where did you get the money from?

HR: I didn't have the money, so I requested Dabboo (Ratnani) that I would make it in films and then I would pay him!

AC: Did you pay him?

HR: I don't think so. Is he here? I will check on that, but I don't think I paid him. So I told my mom about him and at the same time I had done another photo session with Gautam (Rajyadhakshya). Great man! And I was waiting for his pictures as well. So, these were the two big moments which were going to help me decide whether I had it in me or not.

AC: But at the same time there was so much confusion. You have talked about wanting, at some point, to go to Switzerland and do hotel management.

HR: Ya!

AC: Because your friend was doing that. You went to some polytechnic college to check out special effects courses?
HR: Yeah.

AC: What was that?
HR: It was a scary time of my life. I wanted to be an actor. My father, thinking about the struggle that he'd been through, warned me against it. He said, 'You must have something to fall back upon.' So I said, 'Okay, if I don't work as an actor, what do I do?' Uday Chopra, my best friend, and I were always doing things together. Computer classes, this class, that class. So I got him excited about doing special effects. I said, 'Let's go and do special effects, man. Let's go to America for a year or something like that, and do special effects.'

At that time, special effects to me was just a term. I had an impression of some machine in my head. I could buy that machine, know how to put it on and off and people would come, they would work, life would be set. Very cool idea, simple. I love special effects. I love watching these films with special effects.

And then Mr Kader Khan came into my life. Lovely man. But he made my life hell. He told my father, 'Yaar, if your son wants to go and do special effects, he must go to a Polytechnic college, Bhagubhai. Very close by. Your son must go there.' My dad came home. 'Duggu, you want to do this? You have to go to Bhagubhai.'

'What is Bhagubhai?' I asked. 'It's a polytechnic college. When you come out of this college you will be able to fix an AC. You will be able to fix a fridge.'

Was I supposed to be excited? I didn't want to fix an AC. I didn't want to fix a fridge. I took the car, went to Baghubhai. Very surreptitiously I took the turn, went around the bend and saw the college. I saw the students going inside. They would keep a comb stuck in their ear. They used it to make sure that they looked great when they fixed the fridge. I called up Uday and said, 'Dude, listen, man, I have found the answer. If we have to do special effects, we have to go to Bhagubhai, man. It's super cool, dude! We will be able to do everything! Listen to me, I am here, waiting outside the college. Come now.'

AC: And he came?

HR: Yes, fully excited. He asked where the place was. I said it was right behind his house. We had lived here for the past twenty years and we had no idea it was right behind our house. When he reached, I was figuring out what to tell him to get him excited. There was nothing there. He came and sat next to me. Meanwhile, I was trying to build it up with words. He said, 'I am not going in here. I don't need to go here, yaar. My father is okay. I'll go straight to the special effects thing.'

So this went on for some two-three days. Next day, we cancelled the idea. Then we decided to go to Victoria Jubilee Technical Institute (VJTI). So, we went to town in our car. Since we couldn't find the place, we looked around and found a guy on the street, walking idly. We stopped him and I asked him if he knew where VJTI was. He said, 'Ya, ya. I study there.' And got into the car! Uday and I looked at each other.

I said, 'So, good college?'

He said, 'Yes, very, very good college. You are going for admission?'

I said, 'Ya, both of us.' He said, 'Okay, if you are from the 99-98 percentile, you go to building A. If you are from 97-98, you go here.'

And I was thinking...all nineties, and he stopped between 96 and 97, or something like that. I had 69 per cent and Uday had 70 per cent. So, there we were...70, 69, *toh hai hi nahi yahan pe* (70, 69 is not even considered). So we drove up to VJTI, dropped him off and came back home! This is not happening, we said. It will never happen. My father will have to deal with Kader Khan on his own, some way or the other.

So that was the end of my special effects thing. Then I said, *yeh to nahi hone wala hai* (this isn't going to happen). My father still wants me to find something to fall back upon. I found another friend who was going for hotel management in Switzerland. So I quickly called him and asked, 'Sohail, listen. This hotel management thing, is it good?' He said it was good. I said, 'Where will you stay over there?' Sohail said that they would be staying at this college. 'They have a dorm and stuff. It's nice.'

'So what will happen there?' I asked.

'It's great, man! There's snow and stuff.' I got excited because of the snow, but who did I have as company over there? And then I realized at the end of it all that yaar, I am not interested in all this.

I sat down and thought, 'This is going to weaken me.' Then the revelation happened. 'If I have a safety net, am I truly going to be able to jump across the abyss onto the other side knowing that if I fall I'll be safe?' I said to myself that I didn't need that safety net. In fact, that net was going to be a disadvantage. I wanted to have so much fear, or whatever it is. So much passion, so much aggression, so much frustration, because if I didn't, I would die. There would be no second chance, there is nothing. I have to do it, one way or another.

That's when I went up to my dad and said, 'Papa, you have struggled for twenty years in your life. I am your son. Trust me. This is what I want to do. And I don't want a safety net. In fact, if you give me a safety net, I'll tear it bloody down. I want to know if I have it in me. I want to know if I will be able to fly. I will not be able to fly if you are going to weaken me with the safety net.'

AC: Hrithik, you talked about a revelation. You also had a revelation sometime in 1988 when you did a workshop with Feroz Abbas Khan. This was an acting workshop organized by Anupam Kher, and Feroz was taking it. He said that it was basically a sort of an informal workshop. You, Abhishek (Bachchan) and Uday, were all part of it, and the exercise was that you would pick up whatever things were in the room, cover it with a white sheet. Each student would come in and be told that the white sheet was somebody dead, somebody that they had really loved, and this was their final goodbye. And the student would sit next to this body and do whatever came to him or her naturally. And this is what happened to Hrithik. Let's just listen to how Feroz describes it.

[*Voice of Feroz Abbas Khan*]

In the case of Hrithik, when I did that and turned around, this young man had started howling and crying. So I thought he was getting very affected by this particular exercise. But then it went to a point that he started saying, 'I will not do this; I will not do this.' I went there and held him like a child and I also got worried because I thought something was really damaging him. So I got really concerned. I held him and said, 'Look, this is not real. I am just creating this set of circumstances for you to react to and see how sensitive you are as an actor.' And I didn't know this boy. He was very quiet. It was only later that I realized that he is Pinky and Rakesh's son. I had known Pinky for a very long time. So, personally, I did not know him. But the only thing that I came back saying was that he is really an extraordinarily sensitive human being and an actor who can convert his personal experiences into an extremely powerful performance.'

HR: I learnt that to give some of your most fantastic performances as an actor, you have to be lucky. Lucky enough to have gone through experiences in your life that defied everything that you believed in and that questioned your entire existence. One of the most important tools that you can ever have in your life is the fact that one has to grow with every single experience that one has had in life. No experience is going to be bad unless and until I grow with it and from it. It's here to serve me and if I can overcome and if I can overpower it, it's only going to make me a better man, a stronger man. So, if you want to be a great actor or a great creator, be that in your personal life first. You can never create something that is not inside you.

Every brush stroke of a painter is coming from a place of pure instinct. Your instincts get built because of the way you handle every single experience. Your interpretation of life is going to help to interpret every single line and word that you read in a script. That's what acting is about. It's interpretation. Every actor can read the same line and say that line. What's the big deal? Why do some hold your attention? Why do some inspire you with that same line? Because they are projecting something that they have lived, and it's helping them interpret the line in that way.

On that day, I remember, all my friends were there. This was a great challenge for an actor. Somebody that you love so much is dead and is cut into pieces, and are you going to be able to remove the chaadar (sheet)? Are you going to do that or not? That was the whole scene as far as I can remember. And everybody was preparing. I started to prepare. The moment I started to prepare, I felt something so strong within me about the person that I imagined under the sheet that I had to stop. 'In fact, I had to distract myself from that thought, so I started to whistle and sing.

Uday was like, 'Dude, what is he doing, man?' and Abhishek was saying, 'Dude, get him away, it doesn't work like that.' So they are preparing, and I am singing. When the time came, I clicked on my first actor's moment, and I understood what acting is about. There is an art and then there is a craft. You can develop your skill as much as you want. You can really improve your craft a lot by working hard, by preparing, practising your double takes and doing all that kind of stuff, but the art really is your emotional pool that you dive in and out of in your lives.

So, after that experience, when I read a script now and I go through it, I actually live that part. The only time after that scene where I could re-live that kind of moment was in *Koi Mil Gaya* because from my first film to that film all I did was reference acting. When I started off, it was a lot of projection and less of expression. And with *Koi Mil Gaya*, I had no idea what I was going to do.

My father used to ask me, 'Okay, this is the shot, can you walk from there to here and then say the line?'

I would say, 'Papa, I don't know!'

'What do you mean you don't know? You have to know!'

'I know Papa, but I actually don't know!'

He would say, 'Okay. Let's see what you can do.'

So, the entire film I shot like this. I said dialogues which were not there in the script and I just revelled in that. After the take got over, I didn't know what I had done. The joy! I used to rush to the monitor and watch myself and see what I had done. It was such joy!

AC: But, Hrithik, that projection was fairly successful.

HR: Yes, because I had looked at my exterior. I had told you about the video camera.

AC: Yes (to the audience). Once Rakesh ji confirmed him for the role in *Kaho Naa Pyaar Hai*, Hrithik shot continuously and observed himself. He finally made his debut on 14 January 2000. Now let's look at one moment when we collectively, as a country, went bonkers.

[A clip from the song, 'Ek Pal Ka Jeena' from *Kaho Naa Pyaar Hai* plays.]

You guys remember that? So, of course, *Kaho Naa Pyaar Hai* was a monster hit. It released on 14 January, and on 14 February, Valentine's Day, Hrithik got 30,000 marriage proposals. Two months later, he was on the cover of *India Today*. The headline said 'Heartthrob Hrithik' and then there was mass hysteria for many, many, many months. And then there was a twist in the tale. The films that were released afterwards were middling successes or just outright disasters, and murmurs of dissent began.

In May 2002, *India Today* did another story on Hrithik. This one was titled, 'Is Hrithik Roshan a one-trick pony?' *Showtime* magazine put him on the cover again and said, 'Finished!' Exclamation mark; not a question. They were not asking, they were declaring it. The irony, of course, is that *Showtime* has, since, ceased to exist. But my question, Hrithik, is, how did you process this? How do you go from being a superstar to a has-been in two years?

HR: I remember that day. I saw my picture there—a black and white picture—and it said, 'Finished!' I was like, 'Damn! That's amazing! Yes!'

AC: Why?

HR: Because somebody was saying that I couldn't do it. Look at my experiences, my condition, my mindset. My father said, 'You can't do it'. And that's what charged me up.

AC: That's just what you needed?

HR: That's exactly what I needed. So I was challenging people who said that I can't do it. I had to be the underdog to be able to gain victory. I needed people to say, 'He can't do that.'

AC: It didn't break you in any way?

HR: Not at all. My dad had prepared me for something like this, because he used to use the negative vehicle to empower me. This was what I needed at this point of time. And I felt so much power in my bones. I was unstoppable. I could hear background scores, man... Tan tan tan tan tan tan. I felt amazing that day.

AC: Okay, but what did you feel when you were on the cover of *India Today* as the heartthrob? What does that level of adulation do to an actor? Did you have a moment where you really thought you were God?

HR: The moment you say, 'He is the best, he is God,' I know that am not, man. I don't want to do this. Why are they saying all this to me? I go to my room, lock the door. I don't want it.' Then someone says, 'You know what? I don't think he can do it.

And I'm, like, 'What? *Idhar aa* (Come here)?' So that was my... the paradox of things was such, but through that I learnt. I learnt a lot of things in the past three-four years about weakness and strength. True power really is when it doesn't come from a negative vehicle, but you create it yourself. You don't need someone to tell you that you are not good enough. The idea of power, to have self-worth, is when you can say to yourself, 'This is my worth and this is what I can do and I will goddamn do it to the best of my ability and nobody in this world can stop me.' That is true power.

AC: But the debut of the decade and not one moment of vanity?
HR: Ya, one.

AC: What was it?
HR: One moment of vanity. Not vanity, really, but I mean (I'm a) human being, so...there was this one moment. I went to Gaiety (theatre) to be with the crowd. The crowd was like, 'Aye! You are the actor in the film, no? All the best, man!' After the film got over, there were people all over, and I was like, 'What's happening, man? Dude? Kunnu!' My friend Kunnu (Kunal Kapoor) was there with me. He was like, 'I don't know, man, I don't know. Does this happen? I don't know.' It was like everybody was on top of us. Some people thought he was me, so his shirt got torn.

AC: Kunnu became a superstar as well...!
HR: Yes, but he was not in shape. So, he got even angrier. *'Tere six pack hain...mera paunch* (You have six packs and I have a paunch)!' So, for three hours I couldn't walk out of Gaiety. They had to call the cops. The next show got delayed, and there I was. I had become this superstar, untouchable kind of God and I didn't feel it. No change. I wanted to feel that. I wanted to feel like God. And then in time, I was getting invitations from Prince Charles, from the great Nelson Mandela to represent India for some evening tea and I just said that this is not true. It's not me. I don't feel anything. There was a disconnect between the

person I was and the persona they were seeing. But I didn't do anything. In the meantime, things got worse. There were these priests, sadhus and sants, from all over India.

I particularly remember one day when my grandfather called me up and he said that, there was this high priest from Ambarnath, who was at his bungalow and wanted me to be there for just five minutes. So, I went. They stared at me, came close, ran a hand over my face, nodded their heads and went back to Ambarnath. I was looking at all that and saying, 'Dude! What was that?' I took it all in. Before my release, I had these sadhus and sants who told me that my film was going to be the No. 1 film. No matter what happens, my film has to be the biggest hit because it has to announce the arrival of Hrithik Roshan.

That guy had also told me, 'The climax that you have shot, that you don't like...is going to be re-shot.' I said, 'You're crazy. My father never re-shoots anything. Whatever he has shot will be released. He doesn't believe in re-shoot.'

I wish he had spent some time with Mr Vidhu Vinod Chopra. My shots would have been redone! I would have looked better. So he said, no, it's going to be re-shot. And the climax did get re-shot! Next month, it got re-shot. I said, 'What is happening?' All these guys are saying all the true things. So, anyway, after this, something happened that just completely stumped me. I said, 'Oh my God, dude. Just for a second, what if I am the avatar, man?' Has this ever happened? Has any newcomer made such a mark? Have sadhus and sants come like that on the first day and done this? No, man! What if...? I can feel it, yaar. I have so much goodness in me. I want to make the world a better place.

I called up my friend. 'Hey, Sippy! *Tu kahan hai yaar? Sun main aa raha hoon* (Where are you? Listen, I am coming over).' I went to his house. I sat down with him. Thank God for grounded friends. I said, 'Sippy, yaar. I think there is something going on, man. I think I am...I am this...'

Sippy: '*Kya* (What)?'
Me: 'This? You get reborn and stuff? You heard of all these things, no?'
Sippy: 'What?'
Me: 'No, no! Wait, I am just going to say it. I am an avatar.' He looked at me. '*Idhar aa... Tu avatar hai* (Come here! You are the incarnation of God)?' Then he slapped me hard across my face!
He called up all our friends. Everyone gathered around and they took my case for the next week, calling me avatar! '*Aye avatar, idhar aa. Aye mere joote mein thoda polish, thoda* (Hey avatar, come here. Polish my shoes)... So, anyway, that was that.'

AC: That was it.
HR: That was it. I didn't want to be 'avatar'. *Avatar* was out. I liked being myself. Thank you. That was my one God moment.

AC: But the interesting thing is that in that moment, post the failures, when you were at the lowest you have ever been professionally, you were actually constructing the role that would bring you back. Rohit, in *Koi Mil Gaya*, a grown man with the brain of a twelve-year-old. How did you do that role? How did you completely shut off the surround sound of negativity and then create this?
HR: There was no negativity in my head, to be honest. I didn't feel the negativity because I am not a negative person. If the films were not doing well, people were writing bad things about it, and that's something that is there. I wasn't going to fight it or resist it. So, I would leave that aside, as I had something that I was so passionate about doing. I was doing this character who was an embodiment of my entire childhood, that I had been through.

Koi Mil Gaya made me realize that these were the kind of films I wanted to do. Not these kinds of kids' (films) per se, but the films that engage me to the core. So, there was just so much passion, so much enthusiasm. I remember this day when I came on set and I wasn't prepared to do the scene because there was some miscommunication. My dad was supposed to shoot this scene the next day and now he had shifted it to that day, and I didn't know. I sat in my car and sulked for some two hours. I said I couldn't do this scene. And I had this process with Rohit. I just sprayed his perfume. I am very sensitive where smell is concerned. So I had a particular perfume for Rohit. So you spray it right now, I just might go into that zone again.

AC: So, you have a perfume for each character?
HR: Each character which has been moulded to that extent. So for Rohit I had a perfume. For Altaf, I had a perfume. And so I sprayed that on and then I used to walk around my van. And I kept walking. It was almost like regression. So, I was going back into my childhood, this going and going until I didn't feel it. I just kept walking...I wanted to feel something more. I just kept walking. In that walk, my hands would change, my neck would change; it was just like this transmutation that was happening in the walk, and I used to end up as Rohit. And then, for the entire time on set, I used to be Rohit. Whether I was fighting with someone or... I ate like Rohit. It was just something that I enjoyed.

AC: Your father has been a very key architect in your success. In the book that your sister Sunaina did on him, *To Dad with Love*, you say, 'I was afraid of my father because he was such a strict father and disciplinarian. He had a tough life and wanted his children not to take anything for granted in this world. We knew his mood from the way he walked, and the rustle of his trousers.' So this is a relationship which seems hard, not friendly in that sense. How did you evolve from this into one where both of you were collaborators on so many successful movies?
HR: Yes, my father had a hard life and he was very strict with us and I think that's the only way he knew how to motivate us and make us as strong as he is, because he had dealt with the

world. We were protected. So, protecting us, and at the same time, making us stronger, according to me, was not ideal. To make somebody stronger, you got to throw them out, let them learn on their own. Let them fall on their own, like how he did. That's how you build strength.

AC: But, on a set, how did you go up to this person that you have feared, and then say, 'This is wrong'?

HR: Along with his eyes and his need to succeed or whatever, I also inherited his anger. Thank God for that. For a moment, he used to be like, 'That's not good!' I would not give up. I used to keep at it. I was like, 'No, papa, this is the way it should be done because this shot from here will look great. You cannot sacrifice this. Just look at it.' And he would say, 'I don't think so. I'll shoot it and then you see afterwards.' At this time I was an assistant. But when it came to enthusiastic, passionate work, I was unstoppable and I think that is something that he started to respect. The idea was that either I convince him or he convinces me, and then we move on. So that was one thing that helped us traverse that initial director-assistant relationship.

But I think the greatest revelation to me came, I think, last year. My father had been working so hard all his life, I always wondered when and where I would ever see my father just sit down. I am sure there are so many fathers out there who have been burdened with this incredible amount of responsibility that they have to keep this fire burning. That made me sad. I had never seen my father watch a sunset. I had never seen him take a vacation and I just felt that there was something wrong there. I took it as a responsibility to do what he needed.

So, one day, we were working on *Krrish 3* and he called me up. As an actor, in my father's films, I went beyond, I did the background score and the mixing and the visual effects. So, I was handling all of that with the brain problem that was going through at that point of time. I had a hole in my brain. My head was hurting me no end and I got a call from my dad, saying, 'Duggu, you have not done this and you have not done that.' I was like, 'Shit, man, I am doing everything and he's not saying it. I am going to be forty years old, dude. What's going on here? He has got to change.' So I called him back and I said, 'Papa, I want to take you out.' So, he's like, 'Haan?' 'I want to take you out to dine at a restaurant.'

Until then, my father and I had never sat down with each other and had a conversation. It's been all about respect. When he walked into my room, if I was lying down, I would sit up, because he was approaching. I often wondered why I did that. When my mom came in, I didn't do that, and it felt nice. What was it? It was a regressed, repressed emotion and I needed to deal with it. And so, I took my father out.

I sat him down and I took him through his entire journey. I asked him if he remembered how he used to be and how he felt when he had come to Bombay with just ten rupees in his pocket. And did he realize what he had built? Did he realize the empire he had built? 'Do you know what a great life you have lived? Do you realize what a great man you are? Do you see what a great life you have built for me?' And he was like, *'Haan, haan. Theek hai na, woh toh sab karte hain* (Yes, yes. That's okay. Everyone does that).'

I said, 'No, papa! I am talking about you. It was hard for you.' And I took him through all the chapters of his life. I reminded him that he had a son who had a stutter and yet he chose him, chose to see him as a star! 'You were the first one in the world to see me as a star. You mortgaged your house, cars, didn't tell me. I don't know if I could do that for my children.' I don't know if any father could do that. I mean, anybody else who is a bit more intelligent, for want of a better word, would say, 'Let's make a small film. Let's see if he can recite a dialogue. What if he can't?'

And I said, 'Nobody else could have done that, and you did that for me and I never said thank you, papa. I want to thank you. Thank you for making me what I am, thank you for the trust, for that faith.' And my father started crying. I've never seen tears in my father's eyes my whole life. And here was this man who started crying, which turned into bawling, and I started saying, 'Oops! *Thoda zyada ho gaya kya* (Was it too much)?' I wasn't expecting this.

And then I said, 'Papa, you and I are going to be bloody unstoppable for the next ten years. I am with you and we are going to be unbreakable for the next ten years and you are going to make the best film you have ever made because I am with you.' I had to stop the waiters. I had to get up and give him a big hug. Have you seen my father's eyes? Hitler's eyes! Did you ever see Hitler cry? And not just cry! Howl! And I thought this is an Oscar moment! This is my Oscar!

AC: Well done.
HR: That day changed my life. It changed everything. All my assumptions about myself, about the world, everything changed. It was the one breakthrough moment in my life.

AC: Hrithik, you talked about not focusing on yourself, but we are all extremely focused on you. The conversation around you is so much about your physicality. It's so much about how good-looking you are. Is there a burden to beauty? Do you think that your directors feel they must showcase you in a particular way?
HR: Sure...

AC: I mean you even played a Mughal emperor in Jodhaa Akbar...
HR: Sure, sure...

AC: ...we got that scene where the camera was sort of caressing your body and inviting us to lust after you like Jodhaa was.
HR: That was a great moment! I liked that last look. I know you are watching.

AC: But do you ever get a sense that some directors try and exploit the way you look?

HR: *Exploit kya hai* (What is there to exploit)? I mean, if it's working for your scene, if it's again, as I said, inspiring, if it's adding to the moment, it's not ridiculous. It's not just a random, out of the blue, cut-to-abs. *Thoda zoom kar yaar* (Zoom in a little). As long as it's not that, it's fine.

AC: Hrithik, do your roles leak into your life? You had said often in interviews that you were a different person after doing Ethan Mascarenhas in *Guzaarish*. Is that just that particular film or is it with every movie?

HR: I have often said it, but maybe I haven't been able to word it perfectly when I say that I don't think I am a good actor and the reason I keep saying that is because I can't act. If you give me a line, I don't know how to say the line. Another actor, a theatre actor, will have ten thousand ways to say the line. I can't say the line until I know where this guy is coming from. I can't say the line until I know his journey and I don't...until that. I don't know if I am the best person to say the line, until my journey somewhere, somehow coincides with the emotions of that character. I need to find myself in the roles which I do and I need those roles to add to the person I am, to help me grow. So it's a kind of symbiosis where it's a give and take, and that guy I am playing is a real life guy for me.

AC: But do you take those guys home with you?

HR: Ya, some of them. Some of them stay back for a long time. Like Rohit. I remember I was doing a show. I think it was Screen or Filmfare, and I was playing Rohit on the stage and in the act, my Rohit glasses got misplaced. They were lost under the stage, the underside of the stage, and I stayed back till 3 a.m. or 4 a.m., hunting for the glasses. I couldn't let it go. You can call that an emotional dependency, thinking that if I lose that, then I lose a bit of Rohit.

AC: Hrithik, before you became an actor, you were a director...
HR: I wasn't a director...

AC: You made the making of *Koyla*. Is direction still the end goal?
HR: Maybe, I am not thinking on those lines. It is something that I think will evolve as I have more experience in my life. Direction is something you can't gauge—if you can direct or not. If the director takes a shot and I say, 'You know what? We can take it like this,' that doesn't mean I know more than the director. Direction really, truly, is conception; conceiving from zero. Actors can come in where fifty per cent of the job is done, and then say, 'You know what? Take off the red. What if you have white and have one beam coming from there?' It can look spectacular and the people will say, 'Yaar, he's better.' It's not better. Starting from scratch is something else, and being able to incorporate a few decorative points is something else. But, maybe it's a work in progress.

AC: Sometime in the 1950s, Truman Capote did an interview with Marlon Brando in which Brando talked about how he wanted to give up acting, and he said, 'I've very seriously thought about throwing the whole thing up. The business of being a successful actor. What's the point if it doesn't evolve into anything? Alright, you're a success. At last you're accepted, you're welcome everywhere. But that's it, that's all there is to it. It doesn't lead anywhere. You're just sitting on a pile of candy gathering thick layers of crust. Too much success can ruin you as sure as too much failure.' You've seen multitudes of both.
HR: That's bullshit.

AC: Bullshit?
HR: He's focused on himself. He's looking at his story and saying, now what can I do? I have done this, I have done that. What else is there? This is all a day-night, night-day; it's going on. We are doing this, we are doing that. How does it end? Existential

In Conversation with the Stars

questions. Stop. If you're asking those questions, stop. There are no answers. This is the way it is. This is your world. It is going to go on like this. What are you going to do about it? Are you going to sit and complain, saying, 'This is just going on and on and then we are going to die. *Point kya hai yaar? Beer khol* (What's the point really? Open a beer). F**k it. Just sit on it. To hell with it. What's the point? Are you going to be that guy? Or are you going to say, wait a minute.

So many things that have happened in my life and I have evidence of so many things that have happened in my life that I never imagined could have happened. The most important philosophy that I have stumbled upon in my life through my experiences, through my failures, which I now look back and label as strengths, is, 'Be in action. Be in cause.' Ask the right questions. So, moving forward is the one philosophy that is infallible. It's infallibly true.

AC: So Brando was wrong.

HR: Brando was not wrong. He had a moment of self-indulgence. He did that. Then he'd have a drink, go to sleep. The next morning, he'd be back, I guess.

AC: Thank you, Hrithik.

Unleashing the Hurricane

Abhishek Bachchan

A few weeks before my interview with Abhishek Bachchan, he put up a photo of an empty make-up chair on his Instagram and captioned it: 'Possibly the scariest chair to sit on as of right now. It's taken over two years to get back onto it.' It was his first day on the set of *Manmarziyaan* with Anurag Kashyap, a film that was messy and flawed and glorious, just like its subject—love.

I was meeting Abhishek after a long time, and the *Manmarziyaan* actor talks about his sabbatical from the movies, his big comeback and his experience of working with Kashyap. He also discusses his interest in sports, his illustrious family, and how he is ready to 'unleash the hurricane' as an actor, now that he has tasted blood again.

AC: Abhishek, I'm really happy to be sitting here with you. It feels like it's been years.
AB: It has been. The last time we spoke for an interview was a good seven or eight years ago.

AC: On the first day of the *Manmarziyaan* shoot, you posted a lovely picture of your make-up chair on Instagram. You said it was possibly the scariest chair to be on.
AB: Yes, it was.

AC: Why?
AB: It's a bit of a long story. I didn't do any work for about two years in films, in terms of acting. I just felt I needed to reboot somewhere. I wasn't happy with the kind of work I was doing, not the kind of work that was being offered, but the kind of work I was doing. I felt there was a sense of complacency that had crept into my work ethic, and I've always said that the minute an actor becomes complacent, that's when the decay starts. I think I became very comfortable in the work that I was doing.

But I'm not going to lie. I had a blast. I really enjoyed the films I was doing. I was working with people that I really care for, and really love, and really enjoy collaborating with. And I was making more money than I've made in my entire career put together. But there comes a point in time where I think, as an actor and as a creative person, you need to ask yourself, 'Is this what you really came here to do, and is this what you want to be remembered by?' I think that's very important. It was a very difficult decision for me to take.

AC: But was it like, you sat down and said, 'I'm not going to work anymore'?
AB: No, I didn't say I'm not going to work anymore. I'm an actor. I'm from a film family. I dare say, it's in my blood. And at the end of the day, it's what I love doing, apart from the fact that that's all I know. You come from a film family and that's the environment around the house, that's what wakes you up every morning, that's what fuels your passion... So I have never said I'm going to stop acting. I said I need to reboot, I need to re-evaluate, I need to get back to doing work that scares me, get back to doing work that doesn't allow me to sleep at night. It is very convenient to do

a film which is going to be a ₹100-crore, ₹200-crore, ₹300-crore film, the onus is not on you; somebody else is shouldering the burden. You know that it is going to work wonders.

You can sleepwalk through the film because it is going to work. That's a good space to be in and I'm not going to complain. I did quite a few of those and I'm thankful for them because they are the most successful films I've ever made and I am immensely proud of them. I worked very hard on them, but I know somewhere that I was beginning to get complacent when I was getting offered more and more such films.

AC: Was it too easy?

AB: To give you an example, I did a movie with two people that I love immensely—Farah (Khan) and Shah Rukh (Khan)—called *Happy New Year*, and it's been one of the biggest hits I've ever made or been a part of. It's a film because of which, till date, kids come up to me and call me Nandu Bhide. I'm remembered for it, and I loved making every minute of it.

Shah Rukh is one of the greatest leaders to have in a film unit. He makes sure that you have a lot of fun but he makes sure that you work really hard too. Nandu Bhide was an immensely tough character for me to do and I worked very hard with Farah to get it right. I don't know a guy like Nandu Bhide; I've never done a role like this. I thought, 'Am I going to be able to have that kind of abandon that Nandu Bhide had?' And once it's done and you get a bit of appreciation from your audiences, you get that confidence. But can you get another character like that? And I'm like, 'Okay, I can do this, no problem.'

That was the problem. I wanted to be in a place where I'm saying, 'Oh my God! How am I going to do this?' And I wanted to be scared like I was scared when I was doing *Happy New Year*. That's what the issue was.

It's a kind of duality of an actor; you work hard, when you first come into films, you struggle; you're trying to get a job. You get a job and then you struggle with success or failure and your entire efforts are towards achieving the best that you can achieve, so that there's a level of comfort. And then you reach that level, and you're like, no, wait, I don't want to be comfortable. I want to be uncomfortable.

AC: It is a paradox...
AB: Yeah, it is a paradox for an actor that to be the best that you can be, you have to be at the worst stage that you have been in. So that was the phase I was going through. Luckily, I had a lot of other work simultaneously. I had ventured into sports, which is another passion of mine, and I had a kabaddi team and a football team. I concentrated on that, set up the business for that, all with the endgame, knowing that I needed to make this self-sufficient because I wanted to get back to acting. And in the meantime, I was looking.

AC: But what was it about *Manmarziyaan* that said this is the film you should make a comeback with?
AB: It's a great story. Aanand L. Rai sent me a message that he'd like to meet me for a film he was producing. We set up the meeting and we met. I've known him for very many years and he is a very loving, gregarious character.

AC: Yes, very affectionate.
AB: Yeah, you feel like hugging him all the time. He is very huggable. And he said, there is this film I'm really excited about and I'd like you to hear it. He said, don't ask anything else, just hear it. We set up the meeting and the director couldn't make it. They said just the writer will come, and in walked Kanika Dhillon, who is this young, vivacious, full of life, immensely talented and opinionated young lady. She came and narrated the script to me and we then discussed it, and something about it appealed to me. I made a few notes that I shared with her which she very reluctantly agreed to review. They came back to me, and after that

meeting, I said, 'This is nice, this is working.' But I still had one or two apprehensions. At which point I asked, 'Who is directing this film? Are you directing it, or is Kanika directing? Because I have not met the director.' So he said he wanted Anurag (Kashyap) to direct this film. So I said, 'Hmm, okay.'

I've never worked with Anurag and we've had a bit of a patchy past (*laughs*), which thankfully is behind us now. We have all grown up and matured since.

I think that's when I realized that I was ready to get back in front of the camera. And then Anurag came in. He just blew me away. The perspective that he brought to the script just jumped at me and I said, 'I have to do this.' Dare I say it was possibly the first time I saw a pure director's contribution to a script (where Kanika has written this beautiful script), and Anurag has just taken it to a different level?

AC: And did you get what you wanted?
AB: I got what I wanted. I was speaking to my wife the night before (the shoot), and she asked, 'Why are you still awake?'

I said, 'I don't know what he is going to do tomorrow and I'm really scared.'

And in typical fashion, on the first day of the shoot, we didn't end up shooting. So the nerves became even worse. And then the day came upon me.

We were shooting in a hotel and they had given me a room to get ready. If you look closely, this photograph actually was in the hotel room that I was in. And that was the chair. I was looking at this chair and I just said, 'Oh my God! I haven't sat in one of those in over two years!' It was scary, partially since I didn't know what scene Anurag was going to give me because he had not decided.

AC: So he can throw anything at you?
AB: Yeah, yeah, he is very instinctive. He comes to the set and just feels like doing something. He will take a scene which you've rehearsed and you've learnt and you're ready to go, and suddenly

he says, '*Sir, aise karte hain, Isme ye kaattein hain, ye kaattein hain* (Sir, let's do it like this. Let's crop this and this)...' I'm generally very happy when people cut my dialogues, so that was the only good thing, because he knows what he cuts and then once he has turned the scene on its head, he just allows you to do what you have to do. He was immensely generous with me.

You hear so much about Anurag Kashyap and this cult following he has and you expect him to be a particular way, and he is completely the opposite. He just disarms you with his charm and his love. He just allows you to do what you have to do, and I make fun of him. He says, 'Very good, superb, got it. *Thoda refine karte hain ise* (Let's refine it a little).' That means that you're rubbish and you need to do it better. But he allows the actors to just do what they have to do because he doesn't say 'cut'.

AC: He doesn't?
AB: No, so the first few times, he throws you off balance.

AC: How do you know it's over?
AB: Because you just stop. He does not say cut, and there is this awkward silence. Vicky (Kaushal), Taapsee (Pannu), and I were looking at each other and saying, 'So, how's your morning?' But then you say, 'Okay, this guy is not going to say cut.' Then it takes you back to acting school when you used to do improvisations, and you say, 'Okay, here's the situation. He is not going to say cut, so let's figure out what we are going to do next.'

As a performer, it also helps you learn your character even better, and the characters you're working with. So that's the way I took it and I enjoyed myself. He doesn't say 'cut', but he is very generous as a director and he is very loving towards his actors.

AC: And is it like cycling? You never forget?
AB: No, you never forget. You never forget, because you never know it, to start with. I firmly believe acting can't be taught. You either can act or you can't. You can polish your craft, which I think

is essential. But also, I feel that somewhere there was a certain, how do I put it correctly, emotional bankruptcy. I started feeling as though if one has an emotional scene or a dramatic scene, one has to delve to bring out whatever is inside. After doing it long enough, you just know how to do it and it happens. I don't know if the audience figures it out, but as an actor, you know you are not being genuine about it. It is just a recreation or a reprogramming of something that you just know to do really well.

The fun of it is when you feel it really, and it damages you somewhere. I think that's kind of part of being an actor. The one thing I take away from *Manmarziyaan* is the way Anurag pushed me and the way he made me perform. That is when I realized that 'Okay, I've replenished that masala'. It's there and it's ready to go, you want to do it, and once it is there, the craft comes into it. I've always believed on some level that acting is a bit of a power trip.

AC: What do you mean?
AB: It's about power, because you have something which is raw, which can really damage you and hurt you, and most of the time it ends up doing that, and it's like a volcano. Your emotion is just simmering; it's ready to come out. We actors love shots when we get to scream our lungs out, because you just let out everything; it feels good. The reason I say power is because a true craftsman will never give a hundred per cent of that emotion.

AC: You hold back?
AB: You've got to control it, that's your craft. You have to understand it. I can today be here and be very upset and just let it out. When that emotion comes out in its raw form, it comes out as Abhishek Bachchan; it is not coming out as a character. The power is when you are able to control that anger that's pushing to come out, and you control it and say, 'No, no, you don't come out this way, you do it this way'. So, it's about power.

It's a bit of an ego tussle with your inner self. That's exciting; it's like riding a wave. I think that's the true beauty of acting, and only the greats manage to do it. I think if I have to give you a close example, I'd say I've managed to get off the surf board and I am on the wave. I don't know if I will go down to the bottom, but I've realized that this is the feeling I really enjoy. Then you go onto the next challenge and hope that you can do it again.

AC: You know what I find intriguing, Abhishek, is that actresses take breaks usually for practical reasons. They get married or they're going to have kids. With actors, it's a sort of deeper existential crisis. Like you talked about feeling emotionally bankrupt, or your dad took a five-year break, or Mahesh Babu, the Telugu superstar, took a three-year break at the peak of his career. Why do you think that happens? Why does it sort of burden men more?

AB: I don't think it does. I think, as human beings, be it an actor or an actress, you go through the same emotions—the same fear, lack of confidence, but sometimes it is just a decision you need to take. I think those that do it at the peak of their careers are immensely brave.

I think it is the same for the women as well. You go through the same insecurity, be it a year, be it two years, be it five years, but it is just an attitude.

If you look at an actor who is just fantastic and is just at the top of his game, it's Aamir (Khan). He does a film once every two years. But he's working through these two years and he's got that. And I took those two years off, and I said, so what's the difference? After Aaradhya was born, Aishwarya took a few years off because she wanted to concentrate on our daughter, and when she came back she went through the same insecurities.

AC: Mahesh Babu said that the break really helped him. It gave him clarity, it gave him confidence, it changed his approach to what he does. But I've read a lot of interviews where your dad said that the five-year break was a mistake because by the time he came back, the audience had changed and the industry had changed. What did it do for you?

AB: I'll agree with Mahesh on that. I think it's the best thing I've done in my entire career.

AC: Really?

AB: Yeah, I really do. It just sorted my head out. You know, I think the best thing that I learnt in the last two years is something shocking. I kick myself every morning that I never knew what I didn't want to do. I definitely know what I don't want to do or what kind of work I don't want to do.

AC: So there is full clarity on that?

AB: You're never going to achieve full clarity but it's the correct amount of clarity that you need as an actor. I think somewhere as an actor I've always just coasted along, and there's never really been a plan.

I've just been this excited kid who got the opportunity to make films, which has been his lifelong dream. It's a lot more than that. It kind of shatters a lot of ideal beliefs that you want to hold on to. It's not an ideal place. It's not the best place on earth, but, guess what, utopia does not exist.

You can't just be Mr Nice Guy. You can't say I want to be Mr Nice Guy and then be successful. That's not the way the world works. That's not the way Mother Nature intended it to. You have to sacrifice something to achieve something. You've got to pay your dues.

AC: There are no free lunches?

AB: No free lunches. But as Gordon Gekko said, 'Greed is good.' You don't have to be obnoxious about it, but you have to be selfish about yourself. You have to be selfish about your work. You have to be selfish about your family and most importantly, you have to be selfish about your audience because they are the guys who allow you to do what you do, and you owe them.

I've been very blessed that I have an audience which loves me, which supports me, which have stood with me through thick and thin. You owe them, man. It's not like you carry on doing whatever you want and we will be behind you. No, you owe them. We are a part of cinema. Cinema is because of the audience and you're going to work for them.

AC: But Abhishek, was it hard for the family? Did they wonder what you're doing, especially since Amitji has done the break thing himself?
AB: I think in dad's time it was different. It was 1992 when he took that break. Today, you are a lot more plugged into what's going on. Dad and I have spoken about this a lot and I think the main reason was that he felt he had lost touch with what the audiences wanted.

When he came back, he said, he worked with the same people who were making successful films with him before he left, but it was a different industry. They wanted something else.

I think today you're so well plugged in; information is so much more readily available that you pretty much know what's going on, and like I said, I didn't stop and say I don't want to be an actor anymore. I just said I need to change the kind of films I'm doing.

It took two years for me to get the right film or what I perceived to be the right film. It wasn't like I was on a sabbatical. I was working every day. How is it on the family? I spoke to them, I told them, and they were very supportive. They also knew that I had my sports enterprise which was keeping me busy round the clock as well, so it's not like I wasn't working. I was working, and I was actually working very hard. I'm sure if you just ask my parents, somewhere they were like, 'Okay, one year has gone by, and what's this guy doing?' I think that's a parental instinct.

AC: Yeah, exactly.
AB: My wife was fine because I walk my family through everything that I do, so they were on the same page. My parents never told me, but I'm sure somewhere they said, 'Okay, what are you doing?' So I think there was a big sigh of relief when I left for Amritsar.

AC: You've done very well with the sports teams, with the football

team, especially.
AB: Thank you.

AC: What does sports give you that cinema doesn't?
AB: Sports is a lot like theatre; it's instant. In theatre, you do a good scene and you can see the audience react to you. Similarly, in sports, you have a good match, the result is right there, but for me, it's more spiritual than that. I've always been a sportsman and I've learnt a lot in my life through sports. That is what the spirit of being a sportsman or just being involved in sports teaches you.

Sportsmanship, of course, is about a team playing together, how to deal with a difficult situation and react. Be it kabaddi or football, you could be down 2-1; you need to react, you need to come back and win that match. How do you find that character? How do you show your leadership skills? There are so many things that you can literally draw into real life being an owner of a kabaddi team and a football team. Thankfully, both the teams are winning teams. In kabaddi, I won the first season. In football, I won two.

AC: I saw your pictures with that giant cup.
AB: Yeah, it's pretty big. But there have been seasons where we didn't do well. So how do you bounce back from that? How do you go back to the drawing board and come back with the winning team? How do you mould them into a team? How do you keep inspiring them? So there are so many things, and it's been very rewarding.

AC: I was doing this interview with Aishwarya four or five years ago. I have been talking to her for many years and one of the themes she goes back to often is the middle path. This is the idea of not being swayed by success or bogged down by failure.

I asked her if she ever spoke to you about this middle path and this is what she said. I want to read out the whole thing to you: 'The thing about Abhishek is, there is this fun-loving guy the world gets to see and I get to see as well. He is spirited, the prankster, but he's also a very deep guy. Look at what he is born into. Look at what he's lived with. What he's seen throughout his life and look at what he has quietly stood by and stood tall. An incredibly self-contained life, that in itself speaks volumes for what he is within, and how much metal and strength there is. He might not project it, he might not share it, and I don't think, in fact, he even gives us a glimpse into that intensity. I think some roles allow people to get a sneak peek into that, and that's what simmers, but it's there. I don't need to talk to him about a middle path. I think he's known it all his life.' Is this true?

AB: Oh, that's terribly sweet of her. I've never really thought about that. Life was what it was and is what it is. There are two ways to look at it. As I say this, and I fear that I'll be misjudged, but please, I don't mean this in any arrogant way. Please try and see it from my point of view.

I grew up in a household with two immensely talented and famous artists and all their friends were their colleagues. That is the environment I grew up in and that was my normal. When I was a kid, I thought everybody had people standing outside their house waiting for a glimpse of their father.

When I was sent to boarding school, I got a taste of the normal life or as normal as it could be. That's when I started realizing that it was my world. In those days, we didn't have social media. We weren't allowed to watch television beyond watching the news, and there was only Doordarshan in those days. We were allowed to watch a movie once a week, and that was on Sundays. There was either the Sunday movie on television or once the VHS came up, we watched one of dad's films. So we were pretty cocooned that way. That was our world, so there is no question of a left or a right or a middle path—that's the only world I knew. When you grow up, you have a bit more exposure. When you become a professional yourself is when you start realizing there is all of this and then you start having even more respect for your parents for having found that balance and not allowing that to affect you.

The first time it got to me and it was really weird. I think it was 5 September 2004. *Dhoom* had come out a week before and was declared a big hit. It was my first out-and-out success and Adi (Aditya Chopra) had a huge party at the Marriott. When I walked through the lobby for the first time, people actually started running towards me. I was not used to that. I think that was my first brush with, if I dare say, stardom, and I went nuts that night. I had a lot of fun.

I remember it was very early in the morning when the party got over, and we didn't have a car or anything. From the Marriott to my house is a five-minute walk, so I decided to walk. And a very young Arjun Kapoor, who was still an assistant and a dear friend, was with me, and there was Esha Deol, one of my co-stars in the film.

During that walk, Mumbai was waking up, and I was this rock star. I'd given my hit and I'd arrived. I had this swag, my chest was out. People were stopping their cars, coming out, asking for autographs. Those days, camera phones were just about coming in, so that wasn't really the trend. People were stopping and waving. Honestly, I just felt like a dude!

AC: King of the world.

AB: I remember I walked into my house through the gate, and sent the other two away in my car. And I was like, this is what I was looking for, all these years. I rang the doorbell. I said they are going to open the door, and I'm going to be like a king.

My dad opened the door and he said, 'Ah, beta aa gaya.' And I said, 'Amitabh Bachchan.'

Deflated, right there. That's God. You're nothing, man. So I came home to these guys who are completely normal. Dad came out in his nightgown with his glasses on. He was reading the paper and he said, 'You're home.' I was like, that's greatness. You're nothing. So, it was a reality check.

AC: Very quickly.

AB: Every day. So, I think that's the only time I could have felt weird for those couple of hours. After that, it's just fine. It's not even discussed or thought about, because I think everybody realizes in our family, including me, that at the end of the day, it's what you do in front of the camera that's going to matter.

You do that well, the rest of you would just deal with it, and it's going to go away. It's not going to be there forever unless you're Amitabh Bachchan, and you are seventy-six, and you're still at it. We all hope we can be, but we're not. You know it is going to deplete. We've all been in situations where we've walked into the room and been the centre of attention. You walk into that same room a couple of years later and there's a new kid on the block who is the new sensation, and you're sidelined.

AC: But it's so brutal, Abhishek.

AB: It is brutal. It crushes you, but how nice it is that you are able to come back. That you can control that emotion and say, I'm going to use that in my next shot. But that's the way it is and it's the same for everybody in every field. It's just that we do it on a public platform, so there is a certain masochistic streak about actors. You like to suffer on a public stage, but that's the life you choose.

AC: But listen, you're better at it than many others. I mean, what I really admire is your ability to laugh at yourself. Do you remember when Rajkummar Rao put out that tweet about what if there were no surnames in the world, and you responded with 'No, that's all I've got'?

AB: Let me burst your bubble, that wasn't me.

AC: That wasn't you?

AB: No, that wasn't me. It was great. I have this parody account that a lot of people mistake for me. It's hilarious. But I'll probably say that as well.

AC: You will. I could completely believe that you said that. It felt completely in character with you. So, is it just who you are, or have you had to work at it?

AB: I'm pretty facetious, I think, which kind of goes against me most of the time, but that's just the way I've always been. I don't remember having to work at it. Maybe my sense of humour is a bit warped. I find some of the things funny.

On Twitter, a lot of time I get these guys who like to take a swing at me, and I'm fine with that because I'm here, man, I'm public property. Go for it. But if you're going to take a swing at me, bro, I'm going to swing back, and be prepared for that. It is just that my way of doing it is different.

My sense of wit, or whatever you call it, is different. I have a bit of a wry and dry sense of humour, and at the end of the day, you can't take yourself too seriously. You have to learn to laugh at yourself because they are either going to do it to your face or behind your back, but they *are* going to do it.

AC: Right.

AB: So just enjoy it. Everybody has an opinion and as an actor, and I mean this very seriously... as an actor, it is important to hear everybody's opinion. You shouldn't be arrogant enough to think that you're the best and you know everything and you're correct all the time.

Once in a while it's nice to retort, once in a while it's nice to have some fun with it. It upsets me when somebody writes something negative about me, or they are trying to belittle me, or whatever. I can reply back. I have replied to pretty much everything. I might not believe entirely what they're saying, I might not agree with what they're saying, but I have to remember what they're saying because there's a reason why they're saying it.

AC: So you make a note of it?

AB: I absolutely make a note of it and this is also one of the major reasons why I decided to go into this metamorphosis phase of mine. It's how you want to be remembered. We all want to be remembered. You want to do something that you can leave behind, you want to leave behind a legacy.

These are the things I never thought about before. I started thinking that once I had my daughter. I didn't want to be remembered as a joke, because some people thought that. And I remember many years ago, I can't remember exactly what the person said, but somebody tweeted something, a meme, bringing my daughter into it, and that really upset me. I said, look, you want to take a go at me, I'm perfectly fine with that. Leave my daughter out of it; she has nothing to do with this. She's not on social media, so don't bring her into this. And they responded with, 'No no, we don't think your films are nice.' I said, you don't like my films, cool. Thank you. I will work hard to make sure that I make films that you like, and I really meant that, because each and every one matters.

I genuinely believe that if I can make a difference to just one person in the audience, I've achieved something, maybe not even what I wanted to achieve, but I want to make everyone happy. It made me realize that there is a share of people that might not like your work. So why do they not like my work? What can I do to make them like my work?

AC: So, in the eighteen years that you've been making movies, is there one character or film or a scene where you felt like you really nailed it, where you felt you got closest to the emotion you were trying for?
AB: Several.

AC: What would one be?
AB: Sadly, that lasted till the end of the trials when I first saw the film and the next day I'm like, 'Eh, I could have done better.'

AC: Are you very critical of yourself?
AB: Very critical. I make notes.

AC: About what?
AB: I tried to copy you! I remember we were at the premiere of *Avatar* together and your husband and I were sharing popcorn.

We were, if I'm not mistaken, at the IMAX in Wadala. It first bothered me because we were all wearing 3D glasses and after every three minutes, this one flash of light would come on and I would see you with the pad and this extended lamp, making notes!

AC: (*Laughs*) Yes.

AB: I was, like, what is she doing? And by the end of that, I was like, 'Wow, that's a really good idea!' When you're at a movie, you can't assimilate your thoughts as precisely afterwards because afterwards you're just immersed in the experience. I tried that and I couldn't do it, like keeping notes during the movie. But I review my films very often and I make notes. So even a film where I feel at that point of time I've done a good job, a couple of weeks or months later, I feel that I've fallen short and I could have done much better. I keep finding mistakes. I think that's good. You should find mistakes. It helps you grow.

AC: But do you not ever pat yourself on the back and say, 'Well done, Abhishek?'

AB: No.

AC: Never? Like one performance.

AB: No. I think somewhere as an actor it's not about what you think, it is about what your audience is going to think. So people who are going to watch the film actually are your ultimate test. You could have done your best job, nailed it, and then opening day, fifty lakh. What?!

Being a film actor, at the end of the day, the pat on the back is, I think, what the audience gives you through collections. It's what the critics give you through their reviews. That's what matters, and that's what you are looking for as well. After a while what you think doesn't really matter. So I think it's more about the viewer. I haven't been entirely happy with any of my work, and it is not just about my performance. So what was your best a couple of months ago is not good enough anymore.

AC: Sure, and through these eighteen years, are there any regrets? Are there any decisions you wish you hadn't taken, or roads left untravelled?

AB: The sad part about retrospection is everything seems terrible, because you just find a better way of doing everything. Do I regret making the movies that I made? No, because each and every one was a huge learning experience—the ones that did well, and the ones that didn't do well. Either way, I'm happy I did them because they made me the actor that I am today, and I stand or sit before you today as a result of those films.

A huge regret for me, which I've always been very vociferous about, is, I wish I was more prepared when I first started. I wish I was a more accomplished, more aware, and a more prepared actor when J.P. (Dutta) Saab signed me for *Refugee*. I feel somewhere I could not live up to the expectations that he had for me, and he means a lot to me. J.P. Saab introduced me to this world. He's held my hand through it all, even when we've not been working together. He's been a mentor to me and I just feel that he became my schooling for cinema when I should have already been schooled before I came to him. He has never mentioned it. And I don't think he thinks that way about me. I think his love for me is beyond that, but as his actor, as his boy, I wish I was more prepared when I first came into the industry.

I was just a kid in a candy shop. I was just so happy that finally somebody signed me, and it took me two years. Nobody was signing me. People don't believe this, but it's a fact, and I was just so excited that, 'Oh my God, I've got a job'. I remember coming to your house to screen test for *Mission Kashmir* also, and Vidhu took me to the roof and made me pose with the rose. I still remember I was like, 'What am I doing?'

AC: (*Laughs*)

AB: And, you know, I didn't get the part, which was fine because I think he is just such a lovable guy.

AC: I remember reading about *Samjhauta Express* that you were going to do with Rakeysh Omprakash Mehra.

AB: So, *Samjhauta Express* happened when I was not getting a job and nobody wanted to work with me. I had been to almost every director and producer in the industry that I knew, and even ones I didn't know. It came out of frustration. Rakeysh and I got to know each other after he had done my father's first advertising campaign for BPL. They were very popular, but there was this huge uproar about whether Mr Bachchan should be on television. I was sitting with Rakeysh and I had become friends with him then.

I said, 'It's taken me two years; nobody wants to make a film with me.' He said, 'Yeah, even I want to direct a film, but nobody is funding it.' I said, 'Let's work together,' and we started developing a script. We wrote a script called *Samjhauta Express*, which then we gave to Kamlesh Panday ji to make even better, and a host of other people. Then we took it finally to my dad and said, 'We have written this, and will you produce this in ABCL?' It was still making films in those days, and he said, 'This is rubbish, get out of here.'

AC: (*Laughs*)

AB: I'd grown my hair and my beard. In that film I was going to play a Pakistani terrorist who comes to India in search of his father. I went off to Delhi to be with my sister who was a newly-wed at that point in time. This was, I think, in 1998, and when I landed in Delhi I got a message from Rakeysh, asking me to call him. He said, 'I have got this concept, I've got this idea. I'm so upset we are not making Samjhauta,' and he told me his idea, called 'good versus evil'. I said we've got to do this. Let's take it to dad, and that's what became *Aks*.

I remember it was a couple of days after that, I had come back to Mumbai for a Filmfare awards night, and as any aspiring actor, if you get to accompany anybody, you find a way to get there. I remember, Kirron (Kher) Aunty and Anupam Uncle were going, and they took Sikandar and me. I wore the sherwani I got stitched for my sister's wedding.

AC: No way!

AB: Yeah, yeah. I went, and my parents were coming later. Then I went and sat next to them. And it was the year *Border* was nominated and won all these wonderful awards. It was a great film. And J.P. Saab saw me there and at that point, he was thinking of making a movie called *Aakhri Mughal*.

AC: Right.

AB: And a couple of days later he came home and spoke to my dad. And that's how it started. So J.P. Saab saw me at this award function in a sherwani because I didn't have anything else to wear, and that's how I got my first job.

AC: What a long and winding road!

AB: Yeah, it's been a lot of fun.

AC: So, Abhishek, what's next? Have you signed anything else or is there going to be a long gap again?

AB: No, there won't be a long gap. I've tasted blood again. You remember that feeling, like I said, of how much you enjoy it. So there are several projects which are up for discussion right now. They are all diverse and exciting. To be absolutely honest, I haven't put pen to paper on any of them. They are all films that I want to do, but I think, as any actor would tell you, there is a long journey between 'Okay, I'm saying yes to this film,' and the film actually getting made. There is a huge struggle, and so we are currently struggling with that, but I do hope that the producers will manage to make their announcement.

I've traditionally been very scared of making announcements. There is a bit of superstition that whenever I do that, the films never get made. So, let the producers announce it.

AC: Nice. Thank you. And so good to have you back.

AB: Thank you. I'm glad to be back. Time to unleash the hurricane!